SPECIFIC

Gran Gala		
Green Chartreuse		...eur
Grenadine		Sour mix
Guinness	Midori melon liqueur	Southern Comfort
Heavy cream	Mint leaves	Strawberry liqueur
Irish cream liqueur	Mozart dark chocolate liqueur	Tabasco sauce
Jack Daniel's	Overproof rum	Tequila
Jägermeister	Peach schnapps	Triple sec
Jalapeño pepper slice	Peppermint schnapps	Vodka
Jim Beam	Reposado tequila	Whipped cream
Johnnie Walker	Silver Tequila	Whiskey
Lemon-lime soda	Sloe gin	Whole milk

THE ARCHITECTURE
of the
SHOT

Constructing the Perfect Shot from the Bottom Up

WRITTEN BY PAUL KNORR – ILLUSTRATIONS BY MELISSA WOOD

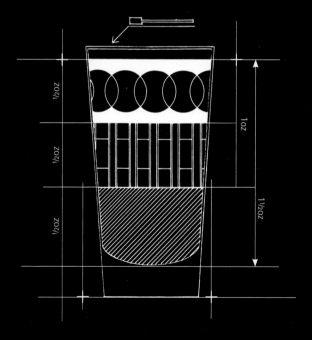

HARPER

HarperCollins*Publishers*
1 London Bridge Street
London SE1 9GF

www.harpercollins.co.uk

First published by HarperCollins*Publishers* 2015

1 3 5 7 9 10 8 6 4 2

© HarperCollins*Publishers* 2015

Paul Knorr asserts the moral right to be identified as the author
of this work

A catalogue record of this book is available from the British Library

ISBN 978-0-00-794492-7

Printed in China

DISCLAIMER:
These recipes all include alcohol. Please drink responsibly.

The recipes included are for batches of 6 shots (for a group), unless otherwise stated.

Some recipes suggest drinking the shots as quickly as possible for enhanced flavor or experience.
Please use your own judgment and drink safely.

A few recipes include open flame. Fire safety tips are included for these drinks, but please apply
caution during preparation.

MIXING SYMBOLS

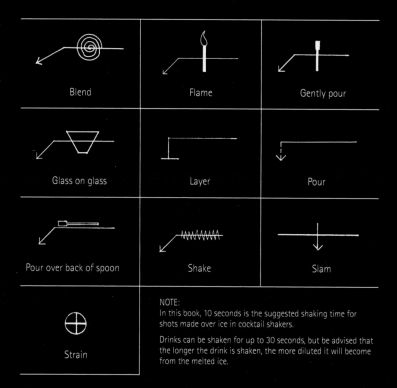

Blend	Flame	Gently pour
Glass on glass	Layer	Pour
Pour over back of spoon	Shake	Slam
Strain		

NOTE:
In this book, 10 seconds is the suggested shaking time for shots made over ice in cocktail shakers.

Drinks can be shaken for up to 30 seconds, but be advised that the longer the drink is shaken, the more diluted it will become from the melted ice.

EMBELLISHMENTS

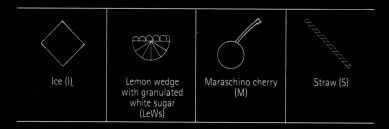

Ice (I)	Lemon wedge with granulated white sugar (LeWs)	Maraschino cherry (M)	Straw (S)

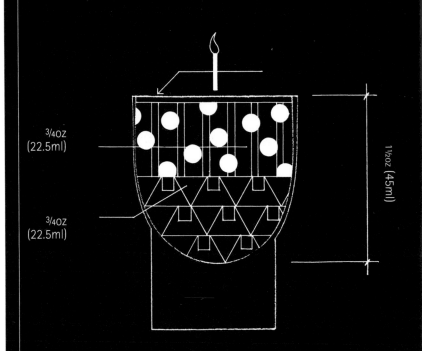

¾OZ
(22.5ml)

¾OZ
(22.5ml)

1½oz (45ml)

AFTERBURNER

Like the roaring flames shooting out the back of an F15 fighter jet, this shot will help the evening take off. In a jet engine the afterburner works by injecting jet fuel into the exhaust *after* the turbine, producing tremendous additional thrust. For those who have tasted overproof (or 151-proof) rum, you know it bears a striking resemblance to jet fuel. At almost double the strength of traditional rum, overproof rum can pack quite a punch. Afterburners on jet engines should be used sparingly as they are inefficient and use up too much fuel. Afterburner shots should *also* be drunk sparingly, so you don't crash and burn early in the evening.

THE NOTES

Make sure that the bar is free of any spilled alcohol by wiping it with a clean cloth and that all napkins and flammable items are at a safe distance. Place six 1½ fluid ounce (45ml) shot glasses on the bar and pour 4½ fluid ounces (135ml) of cinnamon schnapps equally between the glasses. Fill each to the top using 4½ fluid ounces (135ml) of overproof rum. Using a lighter or match, carefully guide the flame to the edge of the glass until the overproof rum ignites. Admire the beauty of an alcohol flame for three to five seconds before snuffing with an inverted pint glass and knocking back the shot.

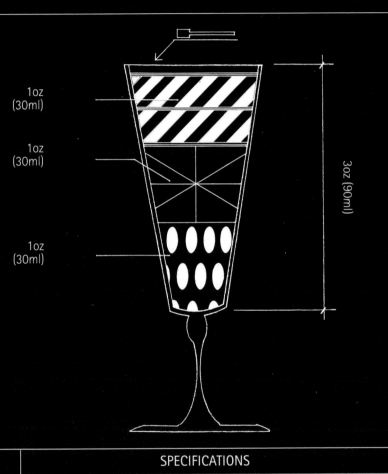

1oz
(30ml)

1oz
(30ml)

1oz
(30ml)

3oz (90ml)

SPECIFICATIONS

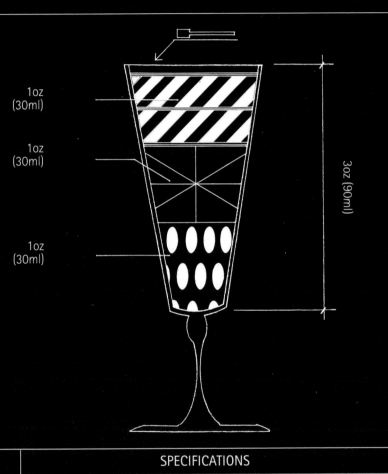 Coffee liqueur

 Peppermint schnapps

Irish cream liqueur

AFTER FIVE

The origin of the After Five shot is steeped in mystery. The most likely theory is that the name refers to the After Eight brand of after-dinner chocolate-covered mints. The eight was replaced with five because, in polite society, drinks should not be served until after 5 P.M. The mix of Irish cream, coffee liqueur, and peppermint schnapps gives the same flavor profile as the delicious chocolates. When these ingredients are carefully layered into a clear shot glass, they form the After Five shot. Of course, this same combination of liqueurs can also be shaken with ice and strained into a shot glass to create another equally sweet, but decidedly more wholesome, shot drink named after a much more well-known brand—the Girl Scout Cookie.

THE NOTES

Pour 1 fluid ounce (30ml) of coffee liqueur into a 3 fluid ounce (90ml) shot glass. Take a long bar spoon and let the edge of the spoon touch just above the coffee liqueur. Slowly pour 1 fluid ounce (30ml) of Irish cream liqueur over the back of the spoon to create a layer. Repeat this process with 1 fluid ounce (30ml) of peppermint schnapps to create a third and final layer.

ALABAMA SLAMMER

The Alabama Slammer is a drink acclaimed by many. NFL quarterback Brett Favre and the University of Alabama have both been associated with the drink's rise to fame. However, long before *The Daily Iowan* credited Favre, this drink featured in the 1980s Tom Cruise movie, *Cocktail*. Going back even further, it can be found listed in the 1971 *Playboy Bartender's Guide*, albeit with a slightly different recipe. Regardless of its origins, this tasty beverage is easy to make and always a crowd pleaser—provided, of course, that your "crowd" is a frat house at the University of Alabama.

THE NOTES

Place 6 or 7 square ice cubes into a cocktail shaker. Pour in 2¼ fluid ounces (67.5ml) of Southern Comfort, coating the ice. Add 2¼ fluid ounces (67.5ml) of amaretto, 2¼ fluid ounces (67.5ml) of sloe gin, and 2¼ fluid ounces (67.5ml) of fresh orange juice. Shake vigorously in a vertical motion for 10 seconds. Strain slowly into six 1½ fluid ounce (45ml) shot glasses. To recreate the movie *Cocktail*, you might choose to flip the bottles over your head and catch them behind your back as you pour. Warning: potentially messy and dangerous, so practice is advised!

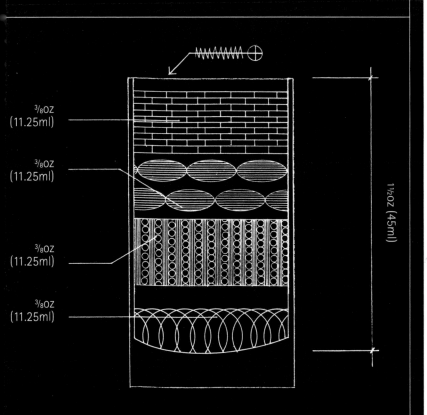

³⁄₈OZ
(11.25ml)

³⁄₈OZ
(11.25ml)

³⁄₈OZ
(11.25ml)

³⁄₈OZ
(11.25ml)

1½OZ (45ml)

SPECIFICATIONS

Southern Comfort

Sloe gin

Amaretto

Fresh orange juice

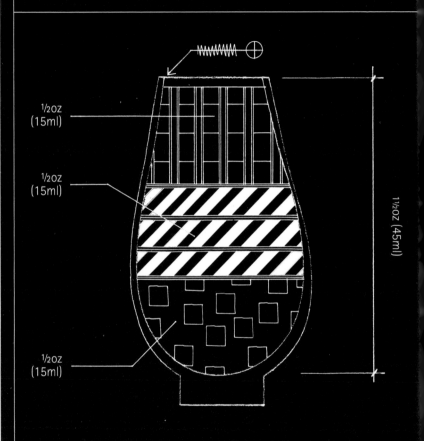

½oz
(15ml)

½oz
(15ml)

1½oz (45ml)

½oz
(15ml)

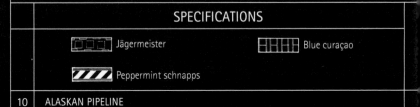

SPECIFICATIONS

Jägermeister

Blue curaçao

Peppermint schnapps

10   ALASKAN PIPELINE

ALASKAN PIPELINE

The Alaskan Pipeline, or more precisely, the Trans-Alaska Pipeline System, is a vast collection of pipelines, feeder pipes, pumping stations, and other sundry parts that together move oil from the far northern part of Alaska near Prudhoe Bay to the ship terminal in Valdez. This shooter gets its name from the fact that it looks (and, some might say, tastes) a bit like crude oil. The deep, dark green of the Jägermeister combines with the glaring fluorescent blue curaçao to make a liquid that is dark indigo in color. The peppermint schnapps increases the viscosity such that it feels almost oily as it slides down the throat.

THE NOTES

Place 6 or 7 square ice cubes into a cocktail shaker. Pour in 3 fluid ounces (90ml) of Jägermeister, coating the ice. Add 3 fluid ounces (90ml) of peppermint schnapps and 3 fluid ounces (90ml) of blue curaçao. Shake vigorously in a vertical motion for 10 seconds. Strain slowly into six 1½ fluid ounce (45ml) shot glasses. To stay authentic to the history of the Trans-Alaska Pipeline System, spill some on the bar before serving.

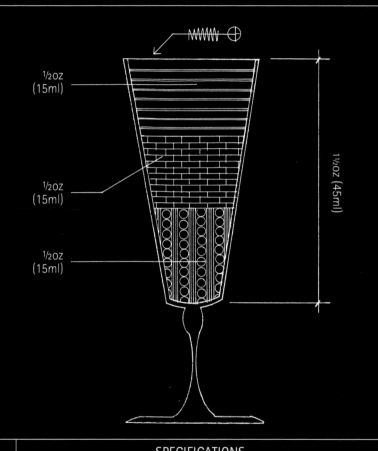

½oz (15ml)

½oz (15ml)

½oz (15ml)

1½oz (45ml)

SPECIFICATIONS

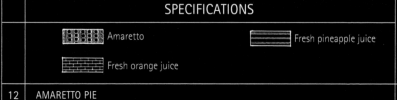

Amaretto

Fresh pineapple juice

Fresh orange juice

AMARETTO PIE

Amaretto is a liqueur that can be found in many mixed drinks because its history stretches back for centuries. The recipe for amaretto liqueur supposedly dates back to the 1500s (see page 15 for the Amaretto Sourball recipe), and many classic cocktails make use of this sweet liqueur. This is not by any stretch of the imagination, a classic. To be frank, this shooter is all about flavor, since the color is an unappealing brownish-muck. The bitter-sweet profile of the amaretto blends here with the acidic tang of the citrus juices to form an odd but pleasing combination.

THE NOTES

Place 6 or 7 square ice cubes into a cocktail shaker. Pour in 3 fluid ounces (90ml) of amaretto, coating the ice. Add 3 fluid ounces (90ml) of fresh orange juice and 3 fluid ounces (90ml) of fresh pineapple juice. Shake vigorously in a vertical motion for 10 seconds. Strain slowly into six 1½ fluid ounce (45ml) shot glasses.

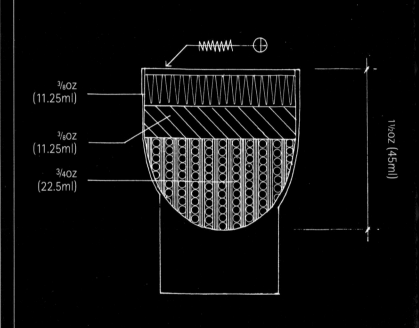

³/₈OZ
(11.25ml)

³/₈OZ
(11.25ml)

³/₄OZ
(22.5ml)

1½OZ (45ml)

SPECIFICATIONS

Amaretto

Vodka

Sour mix

| AMARETTO SOURBALL

AMARETTO SOURBALL

Amaretto is a sweet, syrupy, almond-flavor liqueur, sometimes made from almonds, but more commonly made from apricot pits. This traditional Italian drink's roots can be traced back as far as 1525, if you believe the "meet-cute" love story that Disaronno, the top amaretto producer, has placed on its web site. This disputed tale tells of an artist who falls in love with his model. The woman, being of meager means, gives him a gift of a homemade mixture of apricot pits steeped in brandy. The sour mix in an Amaretto Sourball shot adds a little sour punch to this saccharine story. Sour mix (also called sweet and sour mix) can be made simply, with equal parts sugar and water, and heated in a saucepan until the sugar dissolves. While the simple syrup is still hot, add fresh lemon and fresh lime juice, as it will blend more easily with warm syrup and make for a less cloudy mix. Store in an airtight container and refrigerate for up to 4 weeks.

THE NOTES

Place 6 or 7 square ice cubes into a cocktail shaker. Pour in 4½ fluid ounces (135ml) of amaretto, coating the ice. Add 2¼ fluid ounces (67.5ml) of vodka and 2¼ fluid ounces (67.5ml) of sour mix. Shake vigorously in a vertical motion for 10 seconds. Strain slowly into six 1½ fluid ounce (45ml) shot glasses. Disaronno-brand amaretto contains no nuts and is safe for people with nut allergies.

AMERICAN DREAM

How did this particular combination of ingredients come to be called the "American Dream"? It seems strange since none of them are even remotely native to the United States. Coffee liqueur (especially Kahlúa) hails from Mexico; amaretto and Frangelico are both from Italy; and crème de cacao is French. However, America is renowned for being a melting pot of cultures and tastes, and this drink is a prime example of American cultural fondue.

THE NOTES

Place 6 or 7 square ice cubes into a cocktail shaker. Pour in 2¼ fluid ounces (67.5ml) of coffee liqueur, coating the ice. Add 2¼ fluid ounces (67.5ml) of amaretto, 2¼ fluid ounces (67.5ml) of Frangelico, and 2¼ fluid ounces (67.5ml) of dark crème de cacao. Shake vigorously in a vertical motion for 10 seconds. Strain slowly into six 1½ fluid ounce (45ml) shot glasses. Crème de cacao comes in two varieties: white and dark. The dark crème is, as the name implies, a dark chocolaty-brown, while the white is clear. Surprisingly, they taste about the same, and the choice of white or dark depends on the desired color of the drink. For the American Dream, dark crème de cacao works best alongside the other dark-colored liqueurs.

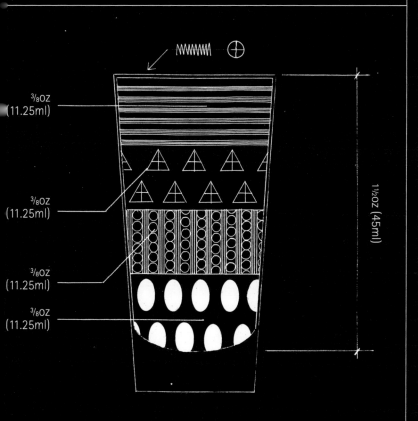

³/₈OZ
(11.25ml)

³/₈OZ
(11.25ml)

³/₈OZ
(11.25ml)

³/₈OZ
(11.25ml)

1½oz (45ml)

SPECIFICATIONS

Coffee liqueur	Frangelico
Amaretto	Dark crème de cacao

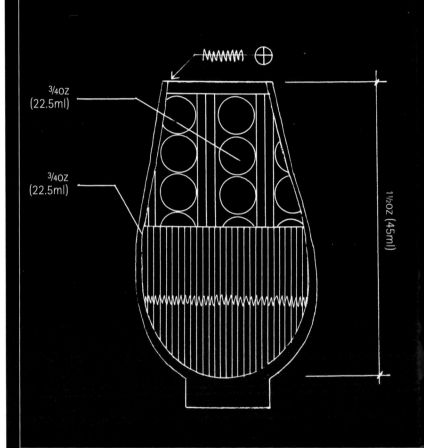

¾OZ
(22.5ml)

¾OZ
(22.5ml)

1½OZ (45ml)

SPECIFICATIONS

Whiskey   Black sambuca

ANACONDA

The name of this drink is presumably supposed to evoke the flavor and sensation of snake venom, alluding to the "bite" you'll receive from its potency. However, the irony is that anacondas are not even venomous—an anaconda actually kills its prey by coiling around and crushing it. Although another possible reason for the name is the crushing headache you will suffer after a night of these, almost as if an anaconda were coiled around your skull.

THE NOTES

First, take a moment to contemplate the life choices that have led you to drink a combination of black sambuca and whiskey. If you still think it's a good idea, proceed to place 6 or 7 square ice cubes into a cocktail shaker. Pour in 4½ fluid ounces (135ml) of whiskey, such as Jack Daniel's, coating the ice. Add 4½ fluid ounces (135ml) of black sambuca. Shake vigorously in a vertical motion for 10 seconds. Strain slowly into six 1½ fluid ounce (45ml) shot glasses. *Are you really sure?*

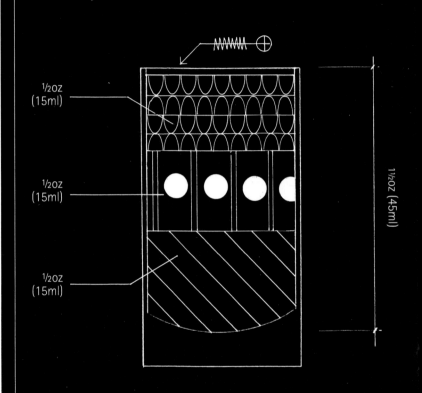

½OZ
(15ml)

½OZ
(15ml)

½OZ
(15ml)

1½OZ (45ml)

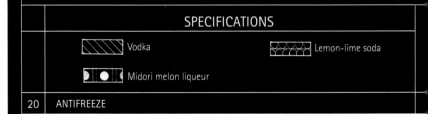

SPECIFICATIONS

Vodka

Lemon-lime soda

Midori melon liqueur

ANTIFREEZE

ANTIFREEZE

Some drinks, such as the Mind Eraser (see page 95), are named for their effect on the person drinking it. Others, such as the Anaconda (see page 19), might allude to the taste of the drink. Then there is the Antifreeze shot—so named purely because its appearance is similar to that of the antifreeze used in car radiators. Ethylene glycol is the most commonly used antifreeze in cars, dyed a bright fluorescent green color to make it easier to spot leaks. This shot gets its bright green color from Midori melon liqueur, a muskmelon-flavored drink. Like its namesake, it's the ideal way to keep you from freezing on cold winter nights.

THE NOTES

Place 6 or 7 square ice cubes into a cocktail shaker. Pour in 3 fluid ounces (90ml) of vodka, coating the ice. Add 3 fluid ounces (90ml) of Midori melon liqueur. Shake vigorously in a vertical motion for 10 seconds. Strain slowly into six 1½ fluid ounce (45ml) shot glasses, filling each one two-thirds of the way full. Fill to the top of each glass using 3 fluid ounces (90ml) of lemon-lime soda.

APOCALYPSE NOW

Apocalypse Now is a world-famous Vietnam War film by Francis Ford Coppola, ranked as one of the top 20 films of all time. The film is noteworthy for its themes of violence and its effect on the human psyche. It is legendary for the troubles experienced during production, ranging from an overweight and unprepared starring actor (Marlon Brando), to expensive sets destroyed by tropical storms. In the movie, a façade of civilization masks the violence behind the Vietnam War and in the shot it is the sweet coffee liqueur and peppermint schnapps that mask the power behind the vodka.

THE NOTES

Place 6 or 7 square ice cubes into a cocktail shaker. Pour in 3 fluid ounces (90ml) of vodka, coating the ice. Add 3 fluid ounces (90ml) of coffee liqueur and 3 fluid ounces (90ml) of peppermint schnapps. Shake vigorously in a vertical motion for 10 seconds. Strain slowly into six 1½ fluid ounce (45ml) shot glasses. Before consuming, wax rhapsodic about how you "love the smell of Napalm in the morning."

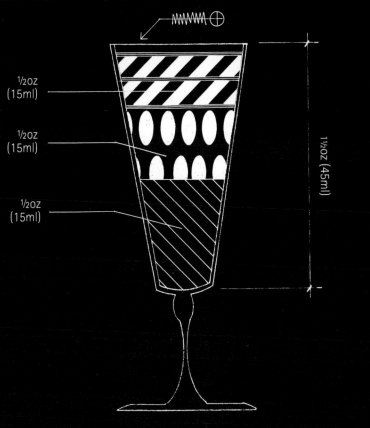

½OZ
(15ml)

½OZ
(15ml)

½OZ
(15ml)

1½oz (45ml)

SPECIFICATIONS

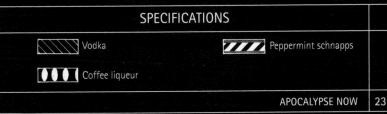

Vodka

Peppermint schnapps

Coffee liqueur

APPLE PIE

The saying "as American as apple pie" is familiar to people around the world, leading them to believe that apple pie is an American invention. This is patently false. First of all, apples themselves are not even American; they were brought over from Europe in the seventeenth century. Written recipes for pies, tarts, and puddings made from apples date as far back as 1381, before America was even discovered! The apple pie familiar to most Americans, with its lattice crust and hint of cinnamon, is actually a variation of a Dutch *appeltaart*. However, over time, American folklore accepted the notion of apple pie as American, and today the U.S. is one of the world's top apple producers. One vague reason for the enduring association of apple pie with Americans is that American GIs during World War II were told to tell reporters "for Mom and apple pie" if asked why they were fighting the war—a stock answer to avoid getting involved in political debates and possible fights. For the Apple Pie shot, the fresh apple juice and cinnamon schnapps combine with the vodka to evoke the flavor of traditional apple pie with a much more powerful kick than the one Grandma used to make.

THE NOTES

Place 6 or 7 square ice cubes into a cocktail shaker. Pour in 4½ fluid ounces (135ml) of vodka, coating the ice. Add 2¼ fluid ounces (67.5ml) of cinnamon schnapps and 2¼ fluid ounces (67.5ml) of fresh apple juice. Shake vigorously in a vertical motion for 10 seconds. Strain slowly into six 1½ fluid ounce (45ml) shot glasses.

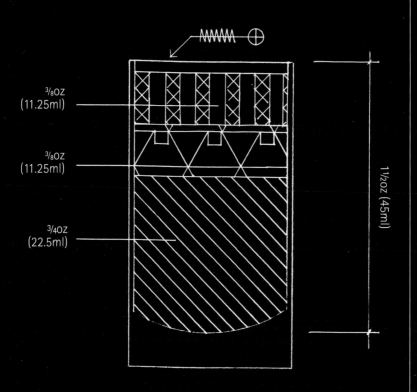

³/₈OZ (11.25ml)

³/₈OZ (11.25ml)

³/₄OZ (22.5ml)

1½oz (45ml)

SPECIFICATIONS

Vodka

Fresh apple juice

Cinnamon schnapps

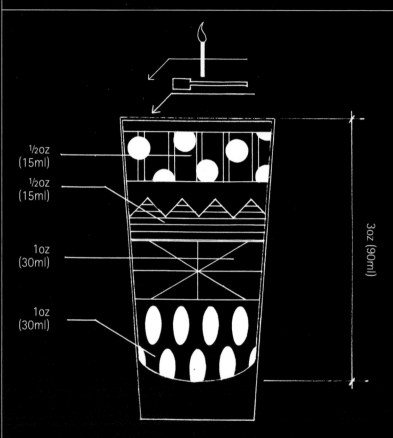

½oz
(15ml)

½oz
(15ml)

1oz
(30ml)

1oz
(30ml)

3oz (90ml)

SPECIFICATIONS

Coffee liqueur	Grand Marnier
Irish cream liqueur	Overproof rum (optional)

B-52
(FLAMING B-52)

Contrary to popular assumption, the B-52 shot is not named after the Boeing B-52 Stratofortress aircraft—at least, not directly. Best known for the song "Love Shack," the B-52s was a new-wave band formed in the late 1970s that took its name from a beehive hairstyle called the B-52. The hairstyle itself was so named because of its resemblance to the front of the B-52 aircraft. Peter Fich, a bartender at the Fairmont Banff Springs Hotel in Alberta, Canada, developed this shot and named it after the band. Mr. Fich was known to name the drinks he invented after the music he liked. To summarize: the shot was named after a band that was named after a hairdo that was named after an aircraft.

THE NOTES

Make sure that the bar is free of any spilled alcohol by wiping it with a clean cloth and that all napkins and flammable items are at a safe distance. Pour 1 fluid ounce (30ml) of coffee liqueur into a 3 fluid ounce (90ml) shot glass. Take a long bar spoon and let the edge of the spoon touch just above the coffee liqueur. Slowly pour 1 fluid ounce (30ml) of Irish cream liqueur over the back of the spoon to create a layer. Repeat this process with 1 fluid ounce (30ml) of Grand Marnier to create a third layer. For a Flaming B-52, reduce the Grand Marnier by half and slowly pour ½ fluid ounce (15ml) of overproof rum over the back of the spoon to create a fourth layer. Using a lighter or match, carefully guide the flame to the edge of the glass until the overproof rum ignites. Admire the beauty of an alcohol flame for three to five seconds before snuffing with an inverted pint glass and knocking back the shot.

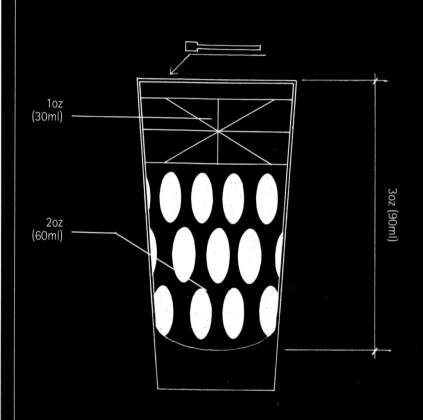

1oz
(30ml)

2oz
(60ml)

3oz (90ml)

SPECIFICATIONS

Coffee liqueur

Irish cream liqueur

BABY GUINNESS

Guinness is an Irish dry stout beer that has been brewed in Dublin, Ireland, since 1759. The most distinctive feature of the beer is the creamy head that forms when a pint of draught is pulled. As the drink settles, a light tan layer of thick foam forms on top of the almost black stout beer. The Irish cream liqueur and coffee liqueur in this shot taste nothing at all like Guinness but when layered in a shot glass, the light tan color of the Irish cream on top of the black color of the coffee liqueur looks like a miniature version of the classic pint. Once it is poured, take the shot in your hand and stomp around like a giant drinking a tiny little beer.

THE NOTES

Pour 2 fluid ounces (60ml) of coffee liqueur into a 3 fluid ounce (90ml) shot glass. Take a long bar spoon and let the edge of the spoon touch just above the coffee liqueur. Slowly pour 1 fluid ounce (30ml) of Irish cream liqueur over the back of the spoon to create a layer. The use of small glasses shaped like pint glasses or miniature beer mugs will enhance the appearance of the shots.

BANANA SPLIT

The banana split sundae was invented by David Evans Strickler in 1904 while he was working at the soda fountain of the Tassel Pharmacy in Latrobe, Pennsylvania. The dessert quickly became popular, spreading across the country and eventually around the world. The sundae consists of a banana split lengthwise with one scoop each of chocolate, vanilla, and strawberry ice cream. The ice cream is then topped with strawberry, pineapple, and chocolate sauces, chopped nuts, whipped cream, and a maraschino cherry. Legend has it that an almost identical ice cream dessert was invented in Boston at about the same time. The crucial difference was that the Boston version featured an unpeeled banana.

The Banana Split shot is a pale recreation of the legendary ice cream treat. Crème liqueurs are very, very sweet liqueurs, and crème de banana and crème de cacao are no exception. At least the sweetness of the liqueurs is cut somewhat by the vodka. The heavy cream adds color and texture to the shot, rather than imparting flavor.

THE NOTES

Place 6 or 7 square ice cubes into a cocktail shaker. Pour in 4½ fluid ounces (135ml) of crème de banana, coating the ice. Add 1½ fluid ounces (45ml) of vodka, 1½ fluid ounces (45ml) of crème de cacao, and 1½ fluid ounces (45ml) of heavy cream. Shake vigorously in a vertical motion for 10 seconds. Strain slowly into six 1½ fluid ounce (45ml) shot glasses.

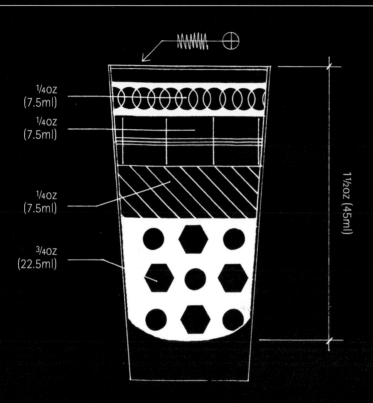

¼OZ
(7.5ml)

¼OZ
(7.5ml)

¼OZ
(7.5ml)

¾OZ
(22.5ml)

1½OZ (45ml)

SPECIFICATIONS

Crème de banana		Crème de cacao	
Vodka		Heavy cream	

BATTERY ACID

Making their appearance in countless movies and comic books, large open vats of acid have often been the mechanism that transforms the bad guy into the super villain. The Battery Acid shot may or may not have the same effect on the person brave enough to consume it. In place of actual acid, the shot is a combination of tequila, green Chartreuse, and overproof rum, which for some can seem equally corrosive. Green Chartreuse is an herbal liqueur made by French monks in the region of Grenoble. It contains over 130 different herbs and plants and is a vibrant green, which gives this shot the green color of a cartoonish battery acid.

THE NOTES

Place 6 or 7 square ice cubes into a cocktail shaker. Pour in 3 fluid ounces (90ml) of tequila, coating the ice. Add 3 fluid ounces (90ml) of green Chartreuse and 3 fluid ounces (90ml) of overproof rum. Shake vigorously in a vertical motion for 10 seconds. Strain slowly into six 1½ fluid ounce (45ml) shot glasses. Purely out of spite and with a healthy disregard for human decency, add 2–3 drops of Tabasco sauce to each shot glass before serving.

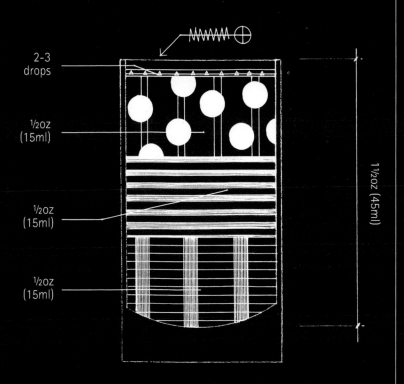

2-3 drops

½oz (15ml)

½oz (15ml)

½oz (15ml)

1½oz (45ml)

SPECIFICATIONS

Tequila

Overproof rum

Green Chartreuse

Tabasco sauce (optional)

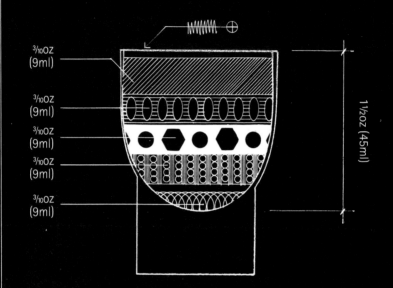

³/₁₀OZ (9ml)
³/₁₀OZ (9ml)
³/₁₀OZ (9ml)
³/₁₀OZ (9ml)
³/₁₀OZ (9ml)

1½oz (45ml)

SPECIFICATIONS

Southern Comfort

Amaretto

Crème de banana

Whole milk

Grenadine

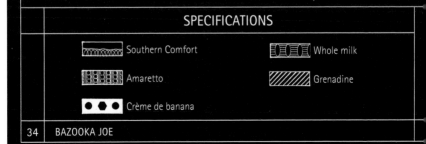

BAZOOKA JOE

Since the 1950s, Topps Bazooka Bubble Gum has come with a small comic strip wrapped inside each piece. The comic featured a cast of characters including the star, Bazooka Joe. Bubblegum comes in many flavors, but the basic "bubblegum flavor" that most people know is a trade secret of the company making the gum. For some strange reason, Southern Comfort, amaretto, and banana liqueur combine to almost exactly replicate the bubblegum flavor. The milk and grenadine are then added to create the distinctive pink color. This is the most popular shot I have had the pleasure to serve. In spite of its bright pink color, everyone enjoys this flashback to their childhood.

THE NOTES

Place 6 or 7 square ice cubes into a cocktail shaker. Pour in 1¾ fluid ounces (52.5ml) of Southern Comfort, coating the ice. Add 1¾ fluid ounces (52.5ml) of amaretto, 1¾ fluid ounces (52.5ml) of crème de banana, 1¾ fluid ounces (52.5ml) of milk, and 1¾ fluid ounces (52.5ml) of grenadine. Shake vigorously in a vertical motion for 10 seconds. Strain slowly into six 1½ fluid ounce (45ml) shot glasses.

BOILERMAKER

The Boilermaker is the original "bomber-style" drink, whereby a shot is dropped into a pint of beer. At some point in the late 1890s or early 1900s, the combination of a shot and a beer came to be known as a "boilermaker." Along with the new name came a new way to drink it. From then on, instead of chasing the whiskey with the beer, the whiskey was dropped *into* the beer, and the entire mixture was consumed in a single (large) gulp. If it was not consumed quickly enough, the beer would foam up and spill out of the glass, making a mess—as well as making the drink a test of stamina and drinking skill.

THE NOTES

Pour 1½ fluid ounces (45ml) of whiskey into a shot glass. Pour 4½ fluid ounces (135ml) of draft beer into a pint glass—pilsners and other light-colored beers work best. When ready to drink, drop the shot into the glass of beer and drink as quickly as you can. Check out the Irish Coffee Drop (see page 79) for a completely different bomber-style drink.

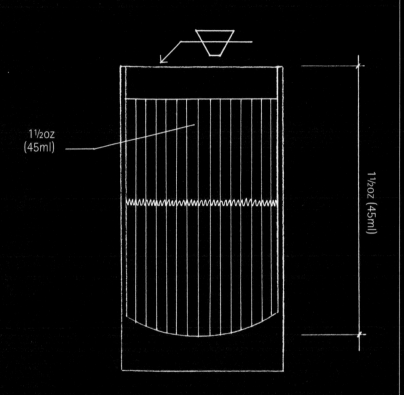

1½oz
(45ml)

1½oz (45ml)

SPECIFICATIONS

Whiskey

Draft beer*
(*To be added to the pint glass)

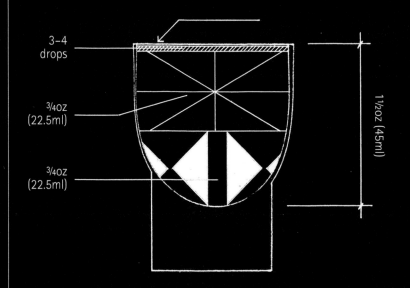

3–4
drops

¾OZ
(22.5ml)

¾OZ
(22.5ml)

1½OZ (45ml)

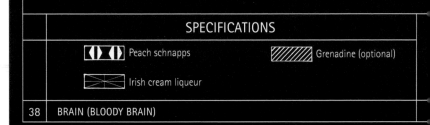

SPECIFICATIONS

Peach schnapps   Grenadine (optional)

Irish cream liqueur

BRAIN
(BLOODY BRAIN)

The Brain shooter, like its cousin the Cement Mixer (see page 43), takes advantage of Irish cream liqueur's tendency to curdle when added to an acidic mixer. In this case, the mixer is peach schnapps. This is a fun drink to serve around Halloween or any other time where a gross or creepy shot is called for (that happens all the time, right?). The Bloody Brain variation simply requires the addition of small drops of grenadine into the center to accentuate the horror.

THE NOTES

Pour ¾ fluid ounce (22.5ml) of peach schnapps into a 1½ fluid ounce (45ml) shot glass. Gently add ¾ fluid ounce (22.5ml) of Irish cream liqueur, allowing it to sink to the middle of the glass and curdle. To make the Bloody Brain, use a dropper or small drinking straw to place 3–4 drops of grenadine into the center of the drink. The grenadine will sink down around the curdled Irish cream, giving it a bloody appearance.

CANDY CORN

Candy corn is to American Halloween what fruitcake is to Christmas. It can be seen everywhere and has become an important touchstone of the season—but finding someone who actually likes the stuff can be a challenge. The comedian Lewis Black has theorized that all of the candy corn in existence was made in 1911 and has been returned and reused since then. Don't worry, he says they wash it each time. The Candy Corn shot actually tastes nothing like the candy, but instead gets its name from the colors of the layers and their resemblance to the tri-colored confection. Licor 43, also known as Cuarenta Y Tres, is a Spanish liqueur flavored with 43 different herbs and spices. The recipe is secret but the most prominent flavor is vanilla. This shot also calls for Gran Gala orange liqueur because of its dark orange color. An alternative orange liqueur can be substituted, provided the color is similar.

THE NOTES

Pour ½ fluid ounce (15ml) of Licor 43 / Cuarenta Y Tres into a 1½ fluid ounce (45ml) shot glass. Take a long bar spoon and let the edge of the spoon touch just above the Licor 43 / Cuarenta Y Tres. Slowly pour ½ fluid ounce (15ml) of Gran Gala over the back of the spoon to create a layer. Repeat this process with ½ fluid ounce (15ml) of heavy cream to create the third and final layer.

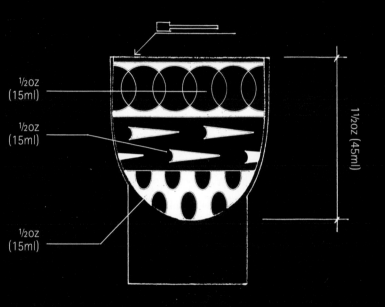

½oz
(15ml)

½oz
(15ml)

½oz
(15ml)

1½oz (45ml)

SPECIFICATIONS

Licor 43 / Cuarenta Y Tres   Heavy cream

Gran Gala

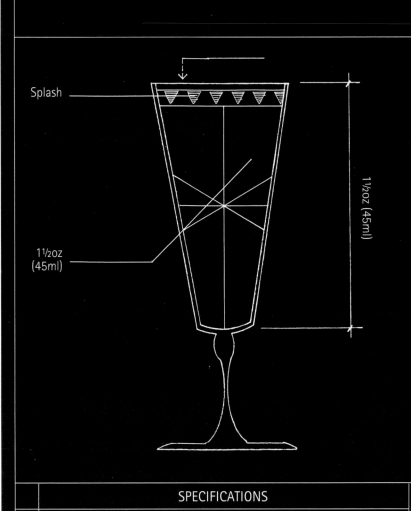

Splash

1½oz
(45ml)

1½oz (45ml)

SPECIFICATIONS

Irish cream liqueur   Fresh lime juice

CEMENT MIXER

As with the Bloody Brain shot (see page 39), the Cement Mixer takes advantage of the unique properties of Irish cream liqueur, specifically its tendency to curdle when in the presence of an acidic mixer. In this case, the combination of Irish cream with the highly acidic fresh lime juice turns the cream into something like the consistency of cottage cheese. If this sounds off-putting or unappetizing, it is meant to be. The Cement Mixer is not supposed to be tasty or enjoyable—rather it is a shot that is given as a challenge to your friends or to the loser of a bet. Once you get past the lumpy, curd-like texture, the flavor of chocolate and lime is actually pretty good.

THE NOTES

Pour 1½ fluid ounces (45ml) of Irish cream liqueur into a 1½ fluid ounce (45ml) shot glass. Carefully add 1 splash of fresh lime juice to the center to curdle the Irish cream.

COPPER CAMEL

True butterscotch candy consists of butter, brown sugar, and treacle boiled together to make a delicious treat. In spite of its lack of any natural ingredients beyond sugar, butterscotch schnapps is quite tasty, evoking the flavor and silkiness of real butterscotch. When combined with the chocolate flavor of the Irish cream, it creates a very simple but delicious shot with the unusual name of the Copper Camel. Legend has it that an unnamed bartender invented the drink for a young female patron and while trying to come up with a name, offered to light her cigarette. He used a copper-colored lighter with the Camel Cigarette logo, and the woman suggested the name "Copper Camel." The best-selling butterscotch-flavored liqueur is called Buttershots and is produced by DeKuyper. This shot is also commonly known as a Buttery Nipple.

THE NOTES

Place 6 or 7 square ice cubes into a cocktail shaker. Pour in 4½ fluid ounces (135ml) of Irish cream liqueur, coating the ice. Add 4½ fluid ounces (135ml) of butterscotch schnapps. Shake vigorously in a vertical motion for 10 seconds. Strain slowly into six 1½ fluid ounce (45ml) shot glasses.

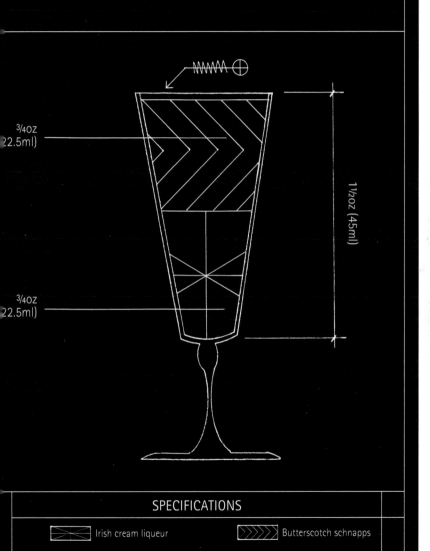

³/₄OZ
(22.5ml)

³/₄OZ
(22.5ml)

1½oz (45ml)

SPECIFICATIONS

Irish cream liqueur   Butterscotch schnapps

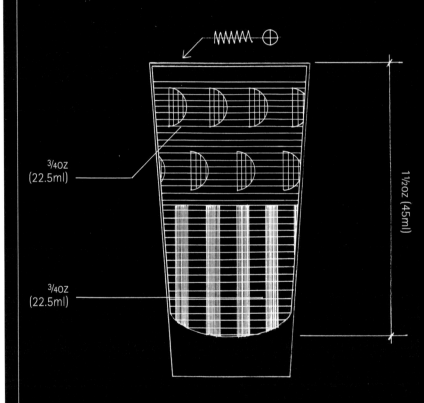

³/₄OZ (22.5ml)

³/₄OZ (22.5ml)

1½oz (45ml)

SPECIFICATIONS

Silver tequila

Lychee liqueur

CROUCHING TIGER

The phrase "Crouching tiger, hidden dragon" is a Chinese idiom describing a place of danger that has its origins in a poem by the sixth-century poet Yu Xin. The phrase was also the title of the Academy Award-winning martial arts movie starring Chow Yun-fat and Michelle Yeoh. The Crouching Tiger shot blends the harshness of silver tequila with the sweet and subtle flavor of lychee liqueur. Silver (or white) tequila comes directly from the still, with none of the aging or mellowing that would be found in gold or reposado tequila. In contrast, lychee liqueur is made from lychee fruit, which have a distinct flavor, often compared to grapes, watermelon, or strawberries. Lychee liqueur used to be very difficult to find, but recently several brands have become more commonly available. Some popular brands include Soho, Paraiso, and Kwai Feh. Bring the tequila and lychee together and it becomes an epic martial arts battle inside your mouth!

THE NOTES

Place 6 or 7 square ice cubes into a cocktail shaker. Pour in 4½ fluid ounces (135ml) of silver tequila, coating the ice. Add 4½ fluid ounces (135ml) of lychee liqueur. Shake vigorously in a vertical motion for 10 seconds. Strain slowly into six 1½ fluid ounce (45ml) shot glasses.

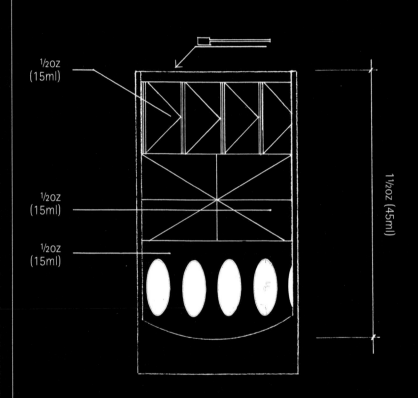

½oz (15ml)

½oz (15ml)

½oz (15ml)

1½oz (45ml)

SPECIFICATIONS

Coffee liqueur

Canadian whiskey

Irish cream liqueur

DUCK FART

The Duck Fart, the signature drink of Alaska, was invented in a bar called the Peanut Farm in Anchorage in 1987. According to the *Alaska Dispatch News*, the drink is quintessentially Alaskan for three reasons: 1) It was invented there; 2) It has an animal in the name; and 3) Its "less-than-genteel name weeds out the delicate." No one seems to remember anymore how the shot arrived at its name, but its popularity quickly took off, with the drink spreading across the country and then around the world. Now there are Duck Fart shot glasses and T-shirts that can be purchased online, all in the name of Alaskan pride. This shot calls for Canadian whiskey, which, because of its high corn content, has a sweeter, mellower flavor than other whiskies.

THE NOTES

Pour ½ fluid ounce (15ml) of coffee liqueur into a 1½ fluid ounce (45ml) shot glass. Take a long bar spoon and let the edge of the spoon touch just above the coffee liqueur. Slowly pour ½ fluid ounce (15ml) of Irish cream liqueur over the back of the spoon to create a layer. Repeat this process with ½ fluid ounce (15ml) of Canadian whiskey, creating the third and final layer.

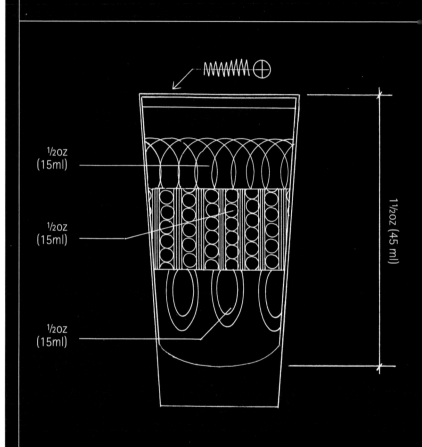

½oz
(15ml)

½oz
(15ml)

½oz
(15ml)

1½oz (45 ml)

SPECIFICATIONS

White sambuca   Southern Comfort

Amaretto

EARTHQUAKE

An earthquake can be a horrifically destructive geologic event and one single earthquake can release energy exceeding that released by a nuclear bomb. The Earthquake shot certainly does not pack as much of a punch as a real earthquake, but it can knock a grown man on his back. The amaretto and Southern Comfort both conspire to mask the power that the white sambuca brings to this drink. Legend has it that this shot was thrown together by a bartender in San Francisco right after the earthquake there in 1989, using the closest unbroken bottles he could find.

THE NOTES

Place 6 or 7 square ice cubes into a cocktail shaker. Pour in 3 fluid ounces (90ml) of white sambuca, coating the ice. Add 3 fluid ounces (90ml) of amaretto and 3 fluid ounces (90ml) of Southern Comfort. Shake vigorously in a vertical motion for 10 seconds. Strain slowly into six 1½ fluid ounce (45ml) shot glasses.

EL VOCHO

El Vocho is the Mexican nickname for a Volkswagen Beetle. These tiny, popular cars can be seen all around Mexico City, with some painted white and green and used as taxis. The El Vocho shot is also white and green and is served in two parts: the shot and the chaser. The shot is simply a shot of reposado tequila, preferably Milagro, served neat. The chaser is a bit more complex and requires some preparation.

THE NOTES

Pour 9 fluid ounces (270ml) each of reposado tequila equally between six 1½ fluid ounce (45ml) shot glasses. Pour 8 fluid ounces (240ml) of fresh pineapple juice into a blender and add 10 fresh cilantro (coriander) leaves, 10 fresh mint leaves, and 1 small slice of jalapeño pepper. Pulse the blender until smooth. Pour into six 1½ fluid ounce (45ml) shot glasses. Place one shot of the chaser next to each shot of tequila.

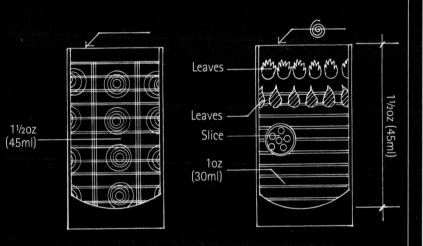

Leaves

Leaves

Slice

1½oz
(45ml)

1oz
(30ml)

1½oz (45ml)

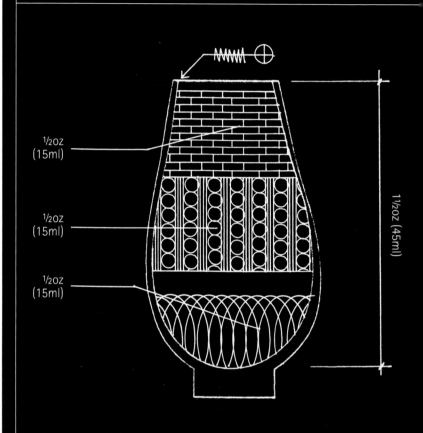

½oz (15ml)

½oz (15ml)

½oz (15ml)

1½oz (45ml)

SPECIFICATIONS

Southern Comfort

Fresh orange juice

Amaretto

ELECTRIC SCREWDRIVER

The classic screwdriver cocktail appears to be an invention of the Smirnoff vodka brand and can be found in their bar guides and sales sheets as the "Famous Smirnoff Screwdriver" as early as 1938. It is possible that the drink existed earlier and that Smirnoff simply used it to promote their vodka, a type of liquor that was not commonly known in the United States at the time. The drink has become a standard that every good bartender knows and can be used as a starting point to create new drinks. There are over one hundred variations of the screwdriver, including this one that substitutes Southern Comfort for vodka and adds some amaretto just for fun.

THE NOTES

Place 6 or 7 square ice cubes into a cocktail shaker. Pour in 3 fluid ounces (90ml) of Southern Comfort, coating the ice. Add 3 fluid ounces (90ml) of amaretto and 3 fluid ounces (90ml) of fresh orange juice. Shake vigorously in a vertical motion for 10 seconds. Strain slowly into six 1½ fluid ounce (45ml) shot glasses.

ESKIMO KISS

Eskimo is considered by some to be an offensive term for the Inuit people of northern Canada, Alaska, and Siberia. An Eskimo kiss is a Westernized version of a traditional Inuit greeting that involves the touching of the tip of one's nose against another's. The actual Inuit *kunik* is an expression of affection between family members and loved ones. To perform a *kunik*, you press your nose and upper lip against the skin of your loved one and breathe in. The Western interpretation of the *kunik* was as a way to kiss without having your lips freeze together. However, the *kunik* actually serves as an intimate way of greeting friends and family when frequently only their nose and eyes were exposed. This shot combines a rich dark chocolate liqueur with a very dry cherry liqueur, with the addition of amaretto to sweeten the deal. The three all come together to create a warm and friendly flavor that would be perfect for old friends to reunite over on a cold winter evening. Mozart dark chocolate liqueur is a truly delicious chocolate liqueur produced in Austria by the Mozart Distillery and can be found in most liquor stores.

THE NOTES

Place 6 or 7 square ice cubes into a cocktail shaker. Pour in 3 fluid ounces (90ml) of Mozart dark chocolate liqueur, coating the ice. Add 3 fluid ounces (90ml) of dry cherry brandy, such as Cherry Heering, and 3 fluid ounces (90ml) of amaretto. Shake vigorously in a vertical motion for 10 seconds. Strain slowly into six 1½ fluid ounce (45ml) shot glasses. Top each shot glass with whipped cream and serve.

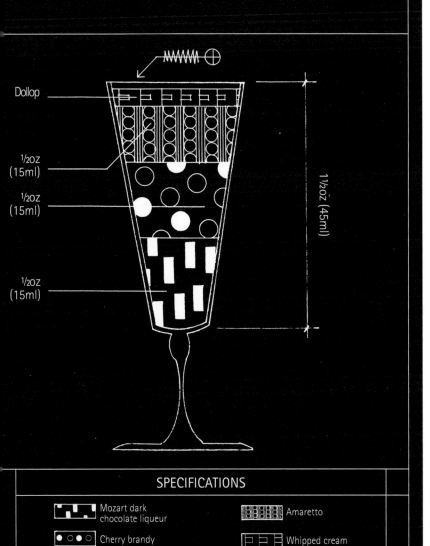

Dollop

½oz (15ml)

½oz (15ml)

½oz (15ml)

1½oz (45ml)

SPECIFICATIONS

Mozart dark chocolate liqueur

Amaretto

Cherry brandy

Whipped cream

ESKIMO KISS | 57

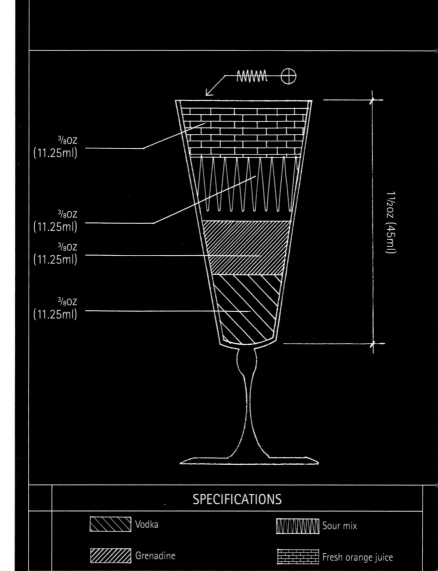

³/₈OZ
(11.25ml)

³/₈OZ
(11.25ml)

³/₈OZ
(11.25ml)

³/₈OZ
(11.25ml)

1½oz (45ml)

SPECIFICATIONS

Vodka

Sour mix

Grenadine

Fresh orange juice

FIFTY-SEVEN CHEVY

The 1957 Chevrolet is considered by many to be an iconic American car. It bears the signature stylistic tail fins of the era, as well as some features considered cutting edge at the time, including tubeless tires. But it was not until the 1960s and 1970s that the popularity of the '57 Chevy really took off. Because of the simplicity of its mechanical design, it was very easy to customize and became a sought-after car for hot rodding. Just like the car, the Fifty-Seven Chevy shot has timeless, stalwart ingredients that leave plenty of room for customization. For example, if orange juice is replaced with pineapple juice, the drink becomes a Fifty-Seven Chevy with Hawaiian Plates. There is another version of this drink meant to be served as a highball or cocktail instead of a shot. This version includes Southern Comfort and sometimes substitutes gin for vodka.

THE NOTES

Place 6 or 7 square ice cubes into a cocktail shaker. Pour in 2¼ fluid ounces (67.5ml) of vodka, coating the ice. Add 2¼ fluid ounces (67.5ml) of grenadine, 2¼ fluid ounces (67.5ml) of sour mix (see page 15), and 2¼ fluid ounces (67.5ml) of fresh orange juice. Shake vigorously in a vertical motion for 10 seconds. Strain slowly into six 1½ fluid ounce (45ml) shot glasses.

FIREBALL

Nello Ferrara created the Atomic Fire Ball candy in 1954 at the height of pop culture's obsession with all things atomic. The bright-red, spicy candy is produced using a hot panning process that builds successive layers, as hot syrup and flavor are added. In Ferrara's candy, the intense cinnamon flavor is not on the outside layer, but on the layer just beneath. The candy starts out sweet like Ferrara's other famous product, the jawbreaker. Once the outer layer begins to dissolve, however, the blast of spicy cinnamon starts to kick in. The Fireball shot works in much the same way—the Southern Comfort acting as the sweet outer layer, delaying the moment when the cinnamon schnapps and the Tabasco start to hit.

THE NOTES

Place 6 or 7 square ice cubes into a cocktail shaker. Pour in 4½ fluid ounces (135ml) of Southern Comfort, coating the ice. Add 4½ fluid ounces (135ml) of cinnamon schnapps. Shake vigorously in a vertical motion for 10 seconds. Strain slowly into six 1½ fluid ounce (45ml) shot glasses. Add 2–3 dashes of Tabasco sauce to each shot glass, allowing it to sink to the bottom. Garnish each glass with a single maraschino cherry to increase the initial hit of sweetness, as well as to represent the candy that was this shot's inspiration.

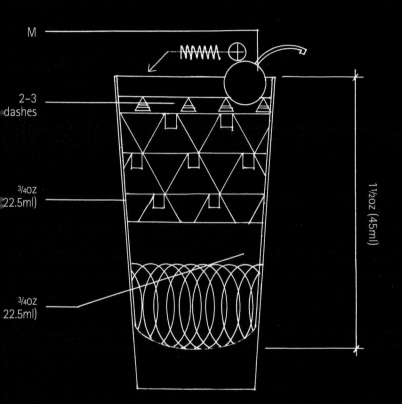

M

2-3
dashes

¾OZ
22.5ml)

¾OZ
22.5ml)

1½oz (45ml)

SPECIFICATIONS		EMBELLISHMENTS	
Southern Comfort	Tabasco sauce	Maraschino cherry (M)	
Cinnamon schnapps			

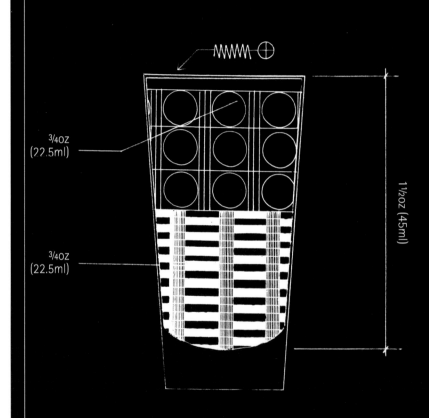

$^3/_4$OZ
(22.5ml)

$^3/_4$OZ
(22.5ml)

1½OZ (45ml)

SPECIFICATIONS	
Gold tequila	Black sambuca

62   FLAT TIRE

FLAT TIRE

For this shot, "flat tire" does not refer to the loss of air in an auto-mobile tire. Instead it refers to a childish prank where someone steps on the heel of the victim's shoe, causing them to trip or the shoe to come off. Like the silly, childish stunt, this shot is meant to lure the uninitiated into drinking a shot with a flavor they were not expecting. The combination of gold tequila and black sambuca can look convincingly—at least in a dark bar—like a shot of whiskey. The flavor, however, is something very different.

THE NOTES

Place 6 or 7 square ice cubes into a cocktail shaker. Pour in 4½ fluid ounces (135ml) of gold tequila, coating the ice. Add 4½ fluid ounces (135ml) of black sambuca. Shake vigorously in a vertical motion for 10 seconds. Strain slowly into six 1½ fluid ounce (45ml) shot glasses.

FOURTH OF JULY

Does this shot really require an explanation? Red, white, and blue are known throughout the world as the colors of the American flag, just as the Fourth of July is known as the date that Americans declared their independence from Britain. But to be historically accurate, July 4 is not actually the correct date. The Continental Congress voted for independence on July 2. The date that stuck was simply a revised wording of the declaration that was approved on the fourth. An excited John Adams wrote to his wife, "The second day of July, 1776, will be the most memorable epoch in the history of America." With its lurid, patriotic hues, a Fourth of July shot will certainly linger in your memory once you've tried one.

THE NOTES

Pour ½ fluid ounce (15ml) of grenadine into a 1½ fluid ounce (45ml) shot glass. Take a long bar spoon and let the edge of the spoon touch just above the grenadine. Slowly pour ½ fluid ounce (15ml) of blue curaçao over the back of the spoon to create a layer. Repeat this process with ½ fluid ounce (15ml) of heavy cream, to create the third and final layer.

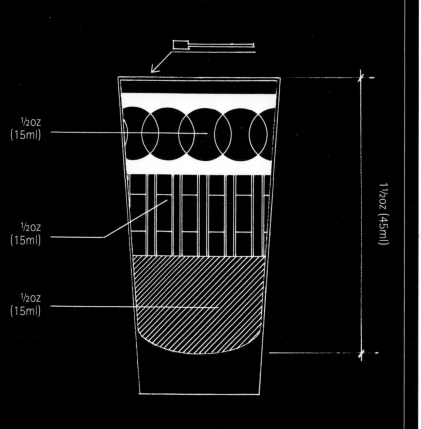

½OZ
(15ml)

½OZ
(15ml)

½OZ
(15ml)

1½oz (45ml)

SPECIFICATIONS

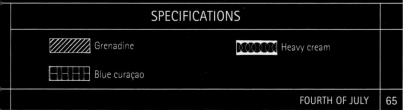

Grenadine

Heavy cream

Blue curaçao

FUZZY NAVEL

The Fuzzy Navel is one of the many drinks invented by bartending legend Ray Foley, in the 1980s. According to one account, Mr. Foley was cutting an orange for garnish when a friend remarked that he could still smell the peach schnapps over the freshly cut orange. The name comes from the fuzziness of the peach, the popularity of navel oranges, and for how the smell of the peach schnapps dominated the drink.

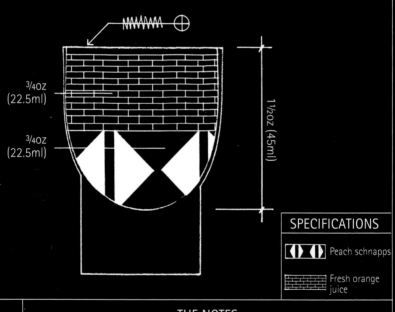

³/₄oz (22.5ml)

³/₄oz (22.5ml)

1½oz (45ml)

SPECIFICATIONS

Peach schnapps

Fresh orange juice

THE NOTES

Place 6 or 7 square ice cubes into a cocktail shaker. Pour in 4½ fluid ounces (135ml) of peach schnapps, coating the ice. Add 4½ fluid ounces (135ml) of fresh orange juice. Shake vigorously in a vertical motion for 10 seconds. Strain slowly into six 1½ fluid ounce (45ml) shot glasses.

GIRL SCOUT COOKIE

The Girl Scouts of America has been selling cookies since 1917 to raise funds for activities, selling over 200 million boxes per year. By far the best-selling variety is the Thin Mint, a chocolate cookie with a mint-flavored chocolate coating, so it is fitting that this shot tastes like the popular cookie in liquid form and is sometimes known as the Thin Mint.

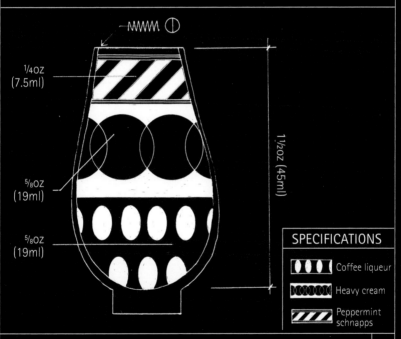

¼OZ (7.5ml)

⅝OZ (19ml)

⅝OZ (19ml)

1½OZ (45ml)

SPECIFICATIONS

Coffee liqueur

Heavy cream

Peppermint schnapps

THE NOTES

Place 6 or 7 ice cubes into a cocktail shaker. Pour in 3½ fluid ounces (105ml) of coffee liqueur. Add 3½ fluid ounces (105ml) of heavy cream and 2 fluid ounces (60ml) of peppermint schnapps. Shake vigorously vertically for 10 seconds. Strain into six 1½ fluid ounce (45ml) shot glasses.

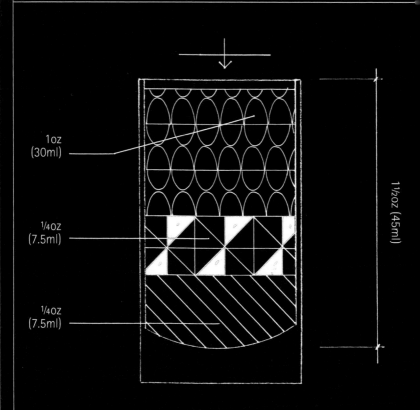

1oz
(30ml)

¼oz
(7.5ml)

¼oz
(7.5ml)

1½oz (45ml)

SPECIFICATIONS

Vodka

Lemon-lime soda

Chambord

GRAPE CRUSH

The Orange Crush Soda Company, in the U.S., was founded in 1916 by Clayton Howell and Neil Ward. They named their company after the patented process that crushed the oranges to extract the essential oils. The brand is now owned by the Dr. Pepper Snapple Group and carries a line of six flavors. The most popular is still orange, but a close runner-up is grape, which was introduced in the 1960s. The Grape Crush shot does not have any actual grape soda in it, but strangely the vodka, raspberry liqueur, and lemon-lime soda combine to produce a drink that both looks and slightly tastes like the grape-flavored Crush soda.

THE NOTES

Pour ¼ fluid ounce (7.5ml) of vodka into a 1½ fluid ounce (45ml) shot glass. Add ¼ fluid ounce (7.5ml) of raspberry liqueur, such as Chambord, and 1 fluid ounce (30ml) of lemon-lime soda, such as Sprite or 7-Up. Now for the fun part: place the palm of your hand tightly over the top of the glass. Raise the glass about 1 foot (30cm) off of the bar top and slam it down hard. The drink will start to foam and should be consumed before it stops foaming.

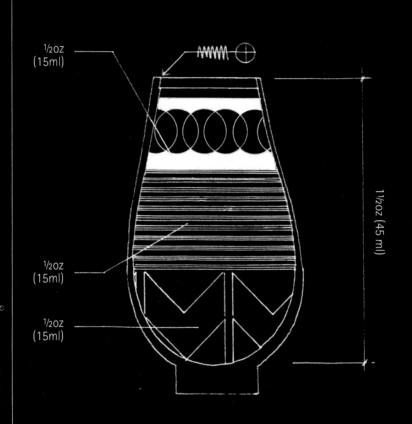

½OZ
(15ml)

½OZ
(15ml)

½OZ
(15ml)

1½oz (45 ml)

SPECIFICATIONS

Green crème de menthe   Heavy cream

Dark crème de cacao

GRASSHOPPER

GRASSHOPPER

The origin of the Grasshopper cocktail is well documented. The drink was created by Philibert Guichet, Jr., the owner of Tujaque's Bar in New Orleans, Louisiana. It was entered in a cocktail contest in New York City, where it won second prize. It is interesting to note that the contest was held in 1928, before the end of Prohibition. The drink derives its name from the green color of the crème de menthe, which was a rare liqueur in 1920s America. By the 1960s, crème liqueurs were much more widely available, and the drink took off in popularity. Traditionally, the drink is served "up" in a cocktail glass but it has also become popular as a shot, with the ratios of the ingredients kept the same.

THE NOTES

Place 6 or 7 square ice cubes into a cocktail shaker. Pour in 3 fluid ounces (90ml) of crème de menthe, coating the ice. Add 3 fluid ounces (90ml) of crème de cacao and 3 fluid ounces (90ml) of heavy cream. Shake vigorously in a vertical motion for 10 seconds. Strain slowly into six 1½ fluid ounce (45ml) shot glasses. Clear crème de cacao can be substituted for the dark version, but the drink should always use the green crème de menthe, or risk losing its iconic color.

HAND GRENADE
(LIT GRENADE)

The Tropical Isle Bar on the corner of Bourbon and Orleans streets in the French Quarter of New Orleans is the "home of the Hand Grenade"—it says so right on the sign. The Tropical Isle Company, which operates several bars on Bourbon Street, has made the drink the center of their marketing strategy, selling souvenir cups, shirts, and hats, as well as a powdered drink mix so you can make Hand Grenades at home. The shot is allegedly the "most powerful drink in New Orleans," although its exact ingredients are a trade secret and the company will go to great lengths to protect their intellectual property. This shot is similar in color and flavor but is in no way associated with Tropical Isle's trademarked product.

THE NOTES

Make sure that the bar is free of any spilled alcohol by wiping it with a clean cloth and that all napkins and flammable items are at a safe distance. Place 6 or 7 square ice cubes into a cocktail shaker. Pour in 3 fluid ounces (90ml) of Midori melon liqueur, coating the ice. Add 3 fluid ounces (90ml) of coconut rum and 3 fluid ounces (90ml) of vodka. Add a splash of fresh pineapple juice. Shake vigorously in a vertical motion for 10 seconds. Strain slowly into six 1½ fluid ounce (45ml) shot glasses. For a Lit Grenade, fill the glass slightly less and float ¼ fluid ounce (7.5ml) of overproof rum on top of each shot. Using a lighter or match, carefully guide the flame to the edge of the glass until the overproof rum ignites. Admire the beauty of an alcohol flame for three to five seconds before snuffing with an inverted pint glass and knocking back the shot.

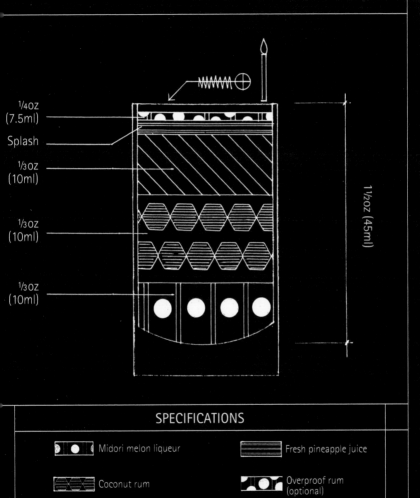

¹/₄oz
(7.5ml)

Splash

¹/₃oz
(10ml)

¹/₃oz
(10ml)

¹/₃oz
(10ml)

1½oz (45ml)

SPECIFICATIONS

Midori melon liqueur	Fresh pineapple juice
Coconut rum	Overproof rum (optional)
Vodka	

HANDS FREE

The Hands Free shot is a drink that is as much about technique as it is about composition. It is made by layering Irish cream and coffee liqueur, much like a Baby Guinness (see page 29) topped with whipped cream. The key part of this shot is in how it is consumed. The person drinking it must place their hands behind their back and work out how to drink it "hands free."

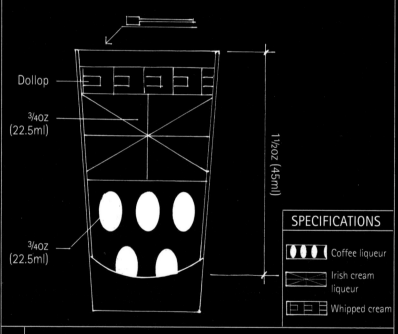

Dollop

3/4OZ
(22.5ml)

1½oz (45ml)

3/4OZ
(22.5ml)

SPECIFICATIONS

Coffee liqueur

Irish cream liqueur

Whipped cream

THE NOTES

Pour ¾ fluid ounce (22.5ml) of coffee liqueur into a 1½ fluid ounce (45ml) shot glass. Position a long bar spoon to touch just above the coffee liqueur. Slowly pour ¾ fluid ounce (22.5ml) of Irish cream liqueur over the back of the spoon to create a layer. Top with whipped cream.

HITS THE SPOT

Chambord is a raspberry liqueur made from red and black raspberries. Its distinctive round bottle can be found behind almost every bar. Chambord's unusual flavor comes from the blend of different varieties of raspberry, as well as the unique manufacturing process, which infuses French cognac, vanilla, and other aromatic herbs. This shot is also known as the G-Spot.

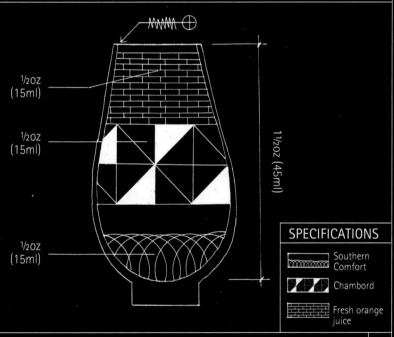

1/2OZ (15ml)

1/2OZ (15ml)

1/2OZ (15ml)

1 1/2oz (45ml)

SPECIFICATIONS

Southern Comfort	
Chambord	
Fresh orange juice	

THE NOTES

Place 6 or 7 ice cubes into a cocktail shaker. Pour in 3 fluid ounces (90ml) of Southern Comfort. Add 3 fluid ounces (90ml) of each Chambord and fresh orange juice. Shake vigorously in a vertical motion for 10 seconds. Strain slowly into six 1 1/2 fluid ounce (45ml) shot glasses.

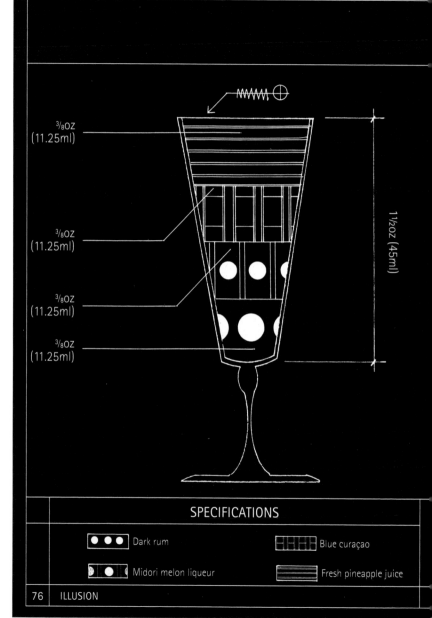

³/₈OZ
(11.25ml)

³/₈OZ
(11.25ml)

³/₈OZ
(11.25ml)

³/₈OZ
(11.25ml)

1½OZ (45ml)

SPECIFICATIONS

● ● ● Dark rum

◖●◗ Midori melon liqueur

▤ Blue curaçao

▬ Fresh pineapple juice

ILLUSION

An illusion is a trick of the senses. Our eyes have a tendency to see what they expect to see, rather than seeing the truth. Magicians take advantage of this in their tricks—just as the Illusion shot fools us with its brown, muddled color into expecting something harsh or strong, when in fact it tastes pretty good. But don't tell anyone what's in it until after they have summoned up the courage to drink it!

THE NOTES

Place 6 or 7 square ice cubes into a cocktail shaker. Pour in 2¼ fluid ounces (67.5ml) of dark rum, coating the ice. Add 2¼ fluid ounces (67.5ml) of Midori melon liqueur, 2¼ fluid ounces (67.5ml) of blue curaçao, and 2¼ fluid ounces (67.5ml) of fresh pineapple juice. Shake vigorously in a vertical motion for 10 seconds. Strain slowly into six 1½ fluid ounce (45ml) shot glasses.

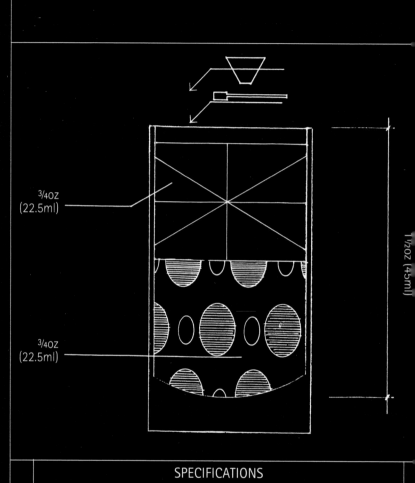

3/4OZ
(22.5ml)

3/4OZ
(22.5ml)

1 1/2OZ (45ml)

SPECIFICATIONS

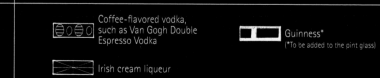

Coffee-flavored vodka, such as Van Gogh Double Espresso Vodka

Irish cream liqueur

Guinness*
(*To be added to the pint glass)

78 | IRISH COFFEE DROP

IRISH COFFEE DROP

Irish coffee was first served in Shannon Airport near Limerick in the 1940s, when passengers coming off a Pan Am Clipper in bad weather were given coffee with a shot of Irish whiskey to warm them up. The drink became world famous when the owner of The Buena Vista Café in San Francisco recreated it in 1952. The Irish Coffee Drop shot takes the traditional Irish coffee recipe and flips it around, using Guinness in place of the coffee and coffee-flavored vodka in place of the whiskey. Now, instead of a warm, soothing drink, you have a raucous shot, similar in technique to a Boilermaker.

THE NOTES

Pour ¾ fluid ounce (22.5ml) of coffee-flavored vodka, such as Van Gogh Double Espresso Vodka, into a 1½ fluid ounce (45ml) shot glass. Take a long bar spoon and let the edge of the spoon touch just above the vodka. Slowly pour ¾ fluid ounce (22.5ml) of the Irish cream liqueur over the back of the spoon to create a layer. Pour half a pint (284ml) of Guinness into a pint glass and allow the beer time to settle. To drink, drop the shot into the glass of Guinness and quaff as quickly as you can.

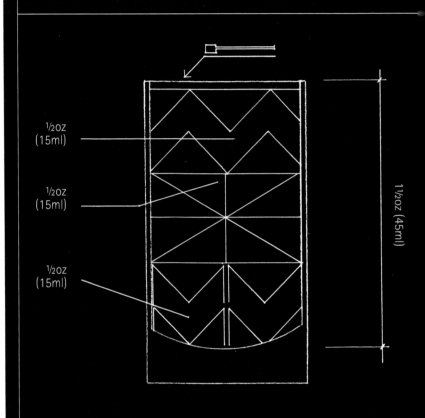

½oz
(15ml)

½oz
(15ml)

½oz
(15ml)

1½oz (45ml)

SPECIFICATIONS

Green crème de menthe

Brandy

Irish cream liqueur

IRISH FLAG

The national flag of Ireland is a vertical tricolor of green, white, and orange. The green represents the Gaelic tradition of Ireland, while the orange represents the Irish followers of William of Orange. The white represents the hope for peace between the two. The flag was first adopted in 1916 by the Easter Rising rebels and was finally given official status in 1937 under the Constitution of Ireland. The Irish Flag shot consequently recreates the three vertical stripes of the flag as horizontal layers in the shot glass. *Sláinte agus táinte!*

THE NOTES

Pour ½ fluid ounce (15ml) of green crème de menthe into a 1½ fluid ounce (45ml) shot glass. Take a long bar spoon and let the edge of the spoon touch just above the green crème de menthe. Slowly pour ½ fluid ounce (15ml) of Irish cream liqueur over the back of the spoon to create a layer. Repeat this process with ½ fluid ounce (15ml) of brandy to create the third and final layer.

JELLY BEAN

According to the National Confectioners' Association, most experts believe the jelly center of a jelly bean is a descendent of the Middle Eastern confection known as Turkish Delight that dates back to Biblical times. Jelly beans come in many flavors, but one of the most iconic is black licorice. Black jelly beans evoke strong feelings in those who try them—most children and many adults avoid them because of their bitter anise flavor. In the Jelly Bean shot, the absinthe provides the strength and the licorice flavor, while the raspberry liqueur and fresh orange juice help to mellow the very intense anise flavor of the absinthe.

THE NOTES

Place 6 or 7 square ice cubes into a cocktail shaker. Pour in 3 fluid ounces (90ml) of absinthe, coating the ice. Add 3 fluid ounces (90ml) of raspberry liqueur (Chambord is recommended) and 3 fluid ounces (90ml) of fresh orange juice. Shake vigorously in a vertical motion for 10 seconds. Strain slowly into six 1½ fluid ounce (45ml) shot glasses. If absinthe is not available, another mild, licorice-flavored liqueur such as Pernod or sambuca can be used instead.

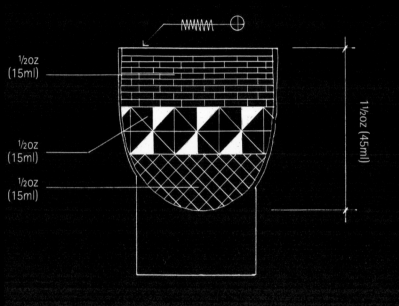

½oz
(15ml)

½oz
(15ml)

½oz
(15ml)

1½oz (45ml)

SPECIFICATIONS

Absinthe

Fresh orange juice

Raspberry liqueur

JOLLY RANCHER

Jolly Rancher hard candies have been around since 1949 and are currently made by the Hershey Company, although they were originally made by the Jolly Rancher Company in Golden, Colorado. The candies come in a wide variety of intense fruit flavors, including grape, sour apple, cherry, watermelon, and blue raspberry. Like its namesake, the Jolly Rancher shot is a sickly sweet-sour taste explosion of brightly colored candy flavors, here made with liqueurs and vodkas.

THE NOTES

Place 6 or 7 square ice cubes into a cocktail shaker. Pour in 1¾ fluid ounces (52.5ml) of cherry-flavored vodka, coating the ice. Add 1¾ fluid ounces (52.5ml) of Midori melon liqueur, 1¾ fluid ounces (52.5ml) of sour apple liqueur, 1¾ fluid ounces (52.5ml) of fresh pineapple juice, and 1¾ fluid ounces (52.5ml) of fresh cranberry juice. Shake vigorously in a vertical motion for 10 seconds. Strain slowly into six 1½ fluid ounce (45ml) shot glasses. This is a standardized version of the shot. The real "recipe" that most bartenders use is to simply add a little bit of every brightly colored liqueur and every candy-flavored vodka they have to hand.

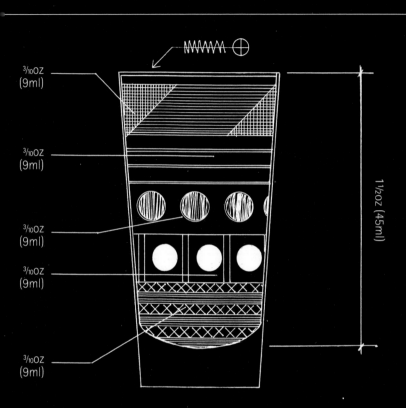

³/₁₀OZ (9ml)

³/₁₀OZ (9ml)

³/₁₀OZ (9ml)

³/₁₀OZ (9ml)

³/₁₀OZ (9ml)

1¹/₂OZ (45ml)

SPECIFICATIONS

Cherry-flavored vodka

Midori melon liqueur

Sour apple liqueur

Fresh pineapple juice

Fresh cranberry juice

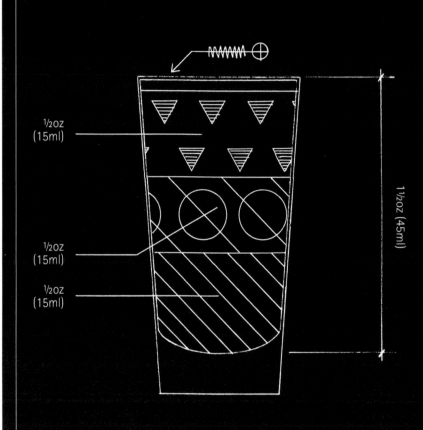

½oz
(15ml)

½oz
(15ml)

½oz
(15ml)

1½oz (45ml)

SPECIFICATIONS

Vodka

Fresh lime juice

Triple sec

KAMIKAZE

The history of shooters can be traced back to the mid-1970s, just as drugs were starting to compete with alcohol as the mind-altering substance of choice. The author Heywood Gould describes the Kamikaze shot perfectly in his 1984 book *Cocktail*: "[The Kamikaze] is one of the classic disco cocktails invented by barbiturated teenagers. It's a senseless, infuriating concoction made of equal parts vodka, lime juice, and triple sec . . . There are no standards for the Kamikaze. It has no particular attributes that would distinguish a good Kamikaze from a bad one, like a dry martini or a tart gimlet. It exists merely to confer a little cache on these pimpled baboons." Enjoy.

THE NOTES

Place 6 or 7 square ice cubes into a cocktail shaker. Pour in 3 fluid ounces (90ml) of vodka, coating the ice. Add 3 fluid ounces (90ml) of triple sec and 3 fluid ounces (90ml) of fresh lime juice. Shake vigorously in a vertical motion for 10 seconds. Strain slowly into six 1½ fluid ounce (45ml) shot glasses. Drink quickly in a "senseless" and "infuriating" manner.

KEY LIME PIE

Key limes are a species of lime introduced to Florida by Spanish explorers. The name refers to the Florida Keys, the chain of islands off the state's southern tip, although the limes are not native to Florida. Key limes differ to regular limes—they have a stronger aroma and a thinner rind. Their zesty juice is the main ingredient in Key Lime Pie, a dessert that originated in Florida's Key West. Key Lime Pie is typically made with a graham cracker crust and for this Key Lime Pie shot, the vanilla and spice flavor of the Licor 43 / Cuarenta Y Tres provides a similar, but sweeter profile against the sharp lime juice. If you can't find Cuarenta Y Tres, use triple sec in its place.

THE NOTES

Place 6 or 7 square ice cubes into a cocktail shaker. Pour in 3½ fluid ounces (105ml) of Licor 43 / Cuarenta Y Tres. Add 3½ fluid ounces (105ml) of heavy cream and 2 fluid ounces (60ml) of fresh lime juice. Shake vigorously in a vertical motion for 10 seconds. Strain slowly into six 1½ fluid ounce (45ml) shot glasses.

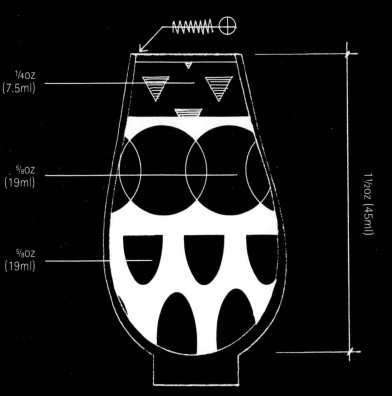

¼OZ
(7.5ml)

⅝OZ
(19ml)

⅝OZ
(19ml)

1½OZ (45ml)

SPECIFICATIONS

Licor 43 / Cuarenta Y Tres

Fresh lime juice

Heavy cream

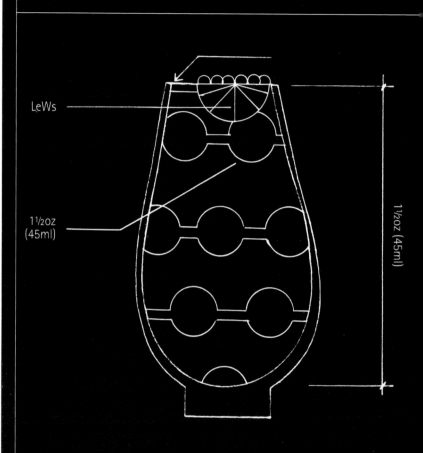

LeWs

1¹/₂oz
(45ml)

1¹/₂oz (45ml)

SPECIFICATIONS	EMBELLISHMENTS
Citrus-flavored vodka	Lemon wedge with granulated white sugar (LeWs)

LEMON DROP

Like many popular shots, the lemon drop is derived from a traditional English candy of the same name. Lemon drop candies are hard, yellow candies flavored with lemon and coated with sugar on the outside. The lemon drop martini is a popular variation on the vodka martini, with fresh lemon juice and confectioners' sugar mixed with the vodka. A lemon drop shot is slightly different to the martini, and, like many other shots, there is a specific ritual that is to be followed. The sugar is used to coat the lemon wedge, the shot of vodka is downed, and then the drinker immediately bites into the lemon.

THE NOTES

Sprinkle 1 teaspoon (5ml) of sugar onto a lemon wedge. Pour a 1½ fluid ounce (45ml) shot of citrus-flavored vodka. Drink the vodka and bite into the sugared lemon wedge.

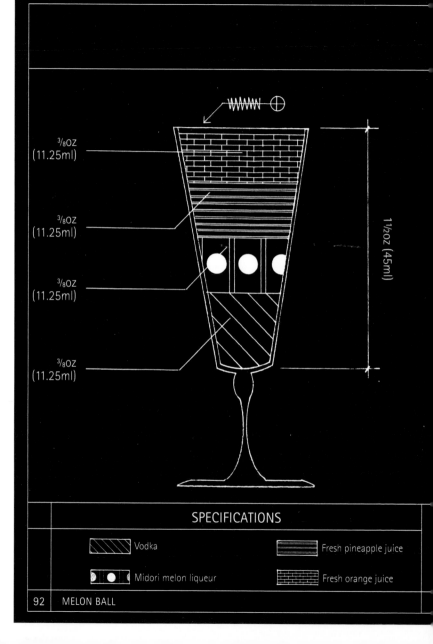

³/₈OZ
(11.25ml)

³/₈OZ
(11.25ml)

³/₈OZ
(11.25ml)

³/₈OZ
(11.25ml)

1½OZ (45ml)

SPECIFICATIONS

◿◿◿◿ Vodka

● ● ● Midori melon liqueur

▬▬▬ Fresh pineapple juice

▦▦▦ Fresh orange juice

MELON BALL

A melon ball is a small round ball of melon, typically honeydew, cantaloupe, or watermelon, which is made with a special utensil called a melon baller. You could use a ball of melon to garnish your shot for extra fun factor. If using a melon ball to garnish, cut each ball about halfway through and slide the ball onto the edge of the shot glass. (But do keep in mind that placing a garnish directly in a shot can be a choking hazard.) The shot has Midori melon liqueur to thank for its melon flavor, as well as for its bright green color. The vodka provides an extra kick, and the fresh pineapple and fresh orange juices make it all taste even fruitier.

THE NOTES

Place 6 or 7 square ice cubes into a cocktail shaker. Pour in 2¼ fluid ounces (67.5ml) of vodka, coating the ice. Add 2¼ fluid ounces (67.5ml) of Midori melon liqueur, 2¼ fluid ounces (67.5ml) of fresh pineapple juice, and 2¼ fluid ounces (67.5ml) of fresh orange juice. Shake vigorously in a vertical motion for 10 seconds. Strain slowly into six 1½ fluid ounce (45ml) shot glasses. Fresh grapefruit juice can be used in place of the pineapple and orange juice for a less-sweet drink.

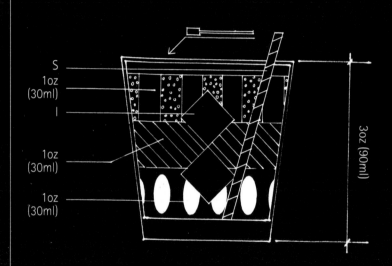

S	
1oz (30ml)	
I	
1oz (30ml)	
1oz (30ml)	

3oz (90ml)

SPECIFICATIONS		EMBELLISHMENTS
Coffee liqueur	Club soda	Straw (S)
Vodka		Ice (I)

| 94 | MIND ERASER |

MIND ERASER

The Mind Eraser is another fun shot that strays from the traditional "shot" format. For this shot, the liquors are layered over ice in a rocks glass, and the whole thing is consumed as quickly as possible through a straw. Pretty clear where the name comes from, is it not? Drinking the shot through a straw gives an alcoholic journey through each of the different layers. First is the sweet and smooth coffee liqueur that coats the mouth and prepares it for what comes next. Then comes the vodka that provides the alcohol burn. Finally, a burst of cool club soda calms everything down and gives the drink a slightly bitter finish. The Six Flags chain of amusement parks has had an inverted steel roller coaster named the Mind Eraser since 1995.

THE NOTES

Place 6 or 7 square ice cubes into a rocks glass or into a large shot glass. Pour in 1 fluid ounce (30ml) of coffee liqueur, coating the ice. Take a long bar spoon and let the edge of the spoon touch just above the coffee liqueur. Slowly pour 1 fluid ounce (30ml) of vodka over the back of the spoon to create a layer. Carefully add 1 fluid ounce (30ml) of club soda to create a third and final layer. Drink as quickly as possible through a straw.

MUD SLIDE

The Mud Slide cocktail dates back to the 1950s and was invented in a bar in the Cayman Islands by a bartender known only as Old Judd. The cocktail was and still is served as a frozen drink when it is not served as a shot. It is also one of the signature drinks of Baileys Irish cream liqueur. Baileys Mudslide mix can be found in half-gallon jugs in many supermarkets.

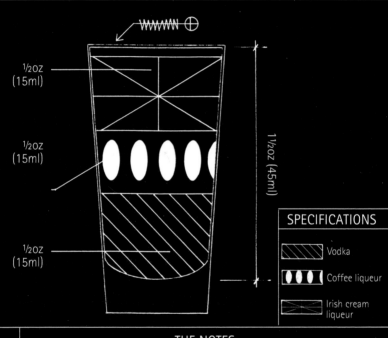

½oz (15ml)

½oz (15ml)

½oz (15ml)

1½oz (45ml)

SPECIFICATIONS

▨ Vodka

◖●●●◗ Coffee liqueur

⬚ Irish cream liqueur

THE NOTES

Place 6 or 7 ice cubes into a cocktail shaker. Pour in 3 fluid ounces (90ml) of vodka. Add 3 fluid ounces (90ml) each of coffee liqueur and Irish cream liqueur. Shake in a vertical motion for 10 seconds. Strain slowly into six 1½ fluid ounce (45ml) shot glasses.

NUTTY IRISHMAN

The Nutty Irishman gets its name from the combination of Irish cream and Frangelico. Frangelico is a hazelnut liqueur whose packaging suggests it is a traditional Italian beverage made for hundreds of years by a remote group of monks—but in fact it was introduced in 1980 by Gruppo Campari. Its nutty flavor is ideal in shots such as the PB&J.

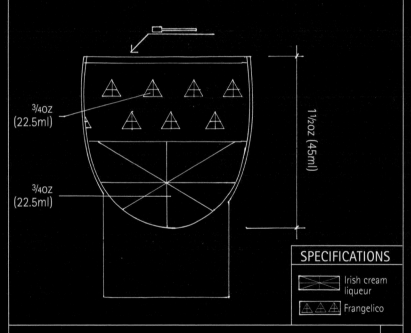

¾OZ (22.5ml)

¾OZ (22.5ml)

1½OZ (45ml)

SPECIFICATIONS

	Irish cream liqueur
	Frangelico

THE NOTES

Pour ¾ fluid ounce (22.5ml) of Irish cream liqueur into a 1½ fluid ounce (45ml) shot glass. Take a long bar spoon and let the edge of the spoon touch just above the Irish cream. Slowly pour ¾ fluid ounce (22.5ml) of Frangelico over the back of the spoon to create a final layer.

OATMEAL COOKIE

In the United States, the oatmeal cookie is second only to chocolate chip as the favorite for homemade cookies. To evoke the flavor of an oatmeal cookie in a shot, Irish cream and heavy cream are combined to give texture, while the coffee liqueur and Frangelico provide flavor. The key to the whole shot, however, is the tiny amount of cinnamon schnapps, giving the drink just the right hint of cinnamon flavor to bring back memories of fresh oatmeal cookies straight out of the oven.

THE NOTES

Place 6 or 7 square ice cubes into a cocktail shaker. Pour in 3 fluid ounces (90ml) of Irish cream liqueur, coating the ice. Add 3 fluid ounces (90ml) of coffee liqueur and 3 fluid ounces (90ml) of Frangelico. Add 1 splash of heavy cream and 1 splash of cinnamon schnapps. Shake vigorously in a vertical motion for 10 seconds. Strain slowly into six 1½ fluid ounce (45ml) shot glasses. The cinnamon schnapps is easy to overdo—add no more than ½ fluid ounce (15ml) for every six shots made. Adjust the amount to taste.

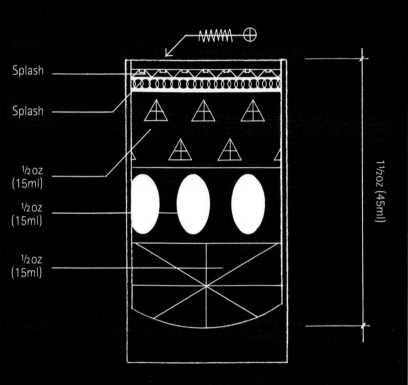

Splash

Splash

1/2 oz
(15ml)

1/2 oz
(15ml)

1/2 oz
(15ml)

1 1/2 oz (45ml)

SPECIFICATIONS

Irish cream liqueur

Coffee liqueur

Frangelico

Heavy cream

Cinnamon schnapps

PB&J

For those without small children or for those not well versed in American food combinations, PB&J stands for peanut butter and jelly and is a simple and easy sandwich, primarily eaten by children. It has been estimated that the average American child will have consumed more than 1,500 PB&J sandwiches by the time they turn 18. Peanut butter is not nearly as popular in Great Britain as it is in the U.S. For those who didn't grow up on peanut butter, the very smell of the stuff can emit instant revulsion in some. But fear not, for the PB&J shot does not contain any actual peanut butter or jelly. Raspberry liqueur, such as Chambord, substitutes for the jelly, in spite of the fact that it is raspberry rather than grape, and Frangelico's hazelnut flavor stands in for the peanut butter. The shot comes together as a whole better than one might expect.

THE NOTES

Place 6 or 7 square ice cubes into a cocktail shaker. Pour in 3 fluid ounces (90ml) of vodka, coating the ice. Add 3 fluid ounces (90ml) of raspberry liquer and 3 fluid ounces (90ml) of Frangelico. Shake vigorously in a vertical motion for 10 seconds. Strain slowly into six 1½ fluid ounce (45ml) shot glasses.

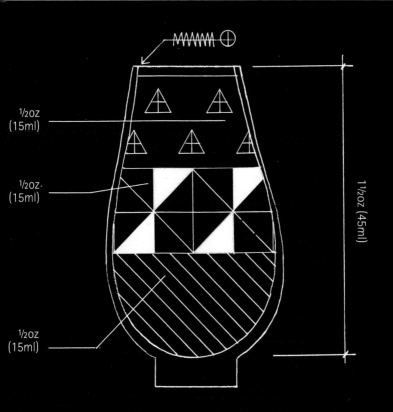

½OZ
(15ml)

½OZ
(15ml)

½OZ
(15ml)

1½OZ (45ml)

SPECIFICATIONS

Vodka

Frangelico

Raspberry liqueur

PEPPERMINT PATTY

The York Peppermint Patty is a sweet peppermint-flavored soft candy enrobed in a bitter dark chocolate that was introduced in 1940 by the York Cone Company in York, Pennsylvania. It has a firm, crisp bite to it, which set it apart from its rivals' soft and gooey centers at the time. It is now made by Hershey's. This shot recreates the flavor of the candy through peppermint schnapps, coffee liqueur, and chocolate syrup.

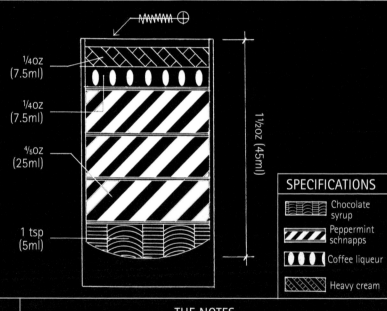

¼oz (7.5ml)

¼oz (7.5ml)

⁴⁄₅oz (25ml)

1 tsp (5ml)

1½oz (45ml)

SPECIFICATIONS

Chocolate syrup

Peppermint schnapps

Coffee liqueur

Heavy cream

THE NOTES

Place 6 or 7 square ice cubes into a cocktail shaker. Add 1 fluid ounce (30ml) of chocolate syrup, 5 fluid ounces (150ml) of peppermint schnapps, 1½ fluid ounces (45ml) of coffee liqueur, and 1½ fluid ounces (45ml) of heavy cream. Shake vigorously in a vertical motion for 10 seconds. Strain slowly into six 1½ fluid ounce (45ml) shot glasses.

PRAIRIE FIRE

Prairie fires are a serious threat in the U.S. Midwest, renowned for their speed and ferocity. The Prairie Fire shot originated in the Midwest as a shot of liquor and hot sauce. It was intended to be downed as punishment for a lost bar bet. There are many variations; this one is also called a Mexican or Texas Prairie Fire, due to the tequila.

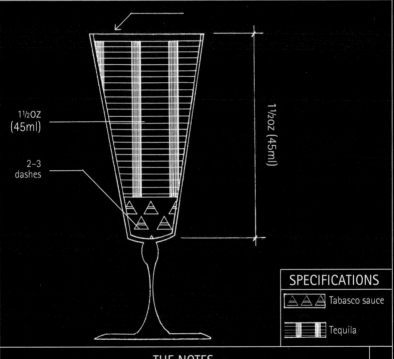

1½OZ
(45ml)

2–3
dashes

1½oz (45ml)

SPECIFICATIONS

△ △ △ Tabasco sauce

Tequila

THE NOTES

Drip 2 or 3 dashes of Tabasco sauce each into six 1½ fluid ounce (45ml) shot glasses. Pour 9 fluid ounces (270ml) of white tequila equally between the glasses.

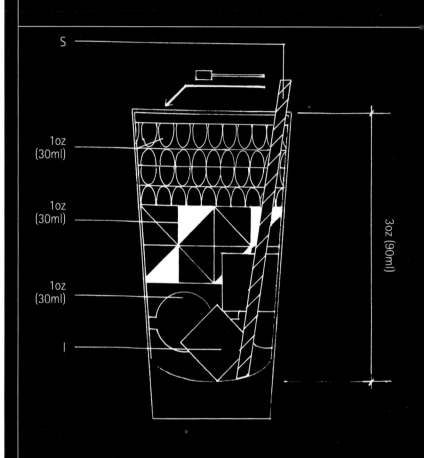

S

1oz
(30ml)

1oz
(30ml)

1oz
(30ml)

I

3oz (90ml)

	SPECIFICATIONS		EMBELLISHMENTS
	Citrus-flavored vodka	Lemon-lime soda	Straw (S)
	Raspberry liqueur		Ice (I)
104	PURPLE HAZE (PURPLE HOOTER)		

PURPLE HAZE
(PURPLE HOOTER)

"Purple Haze" is one of Jimi Hendrix's most famous songs. Released in 1967, the song was assumed to be about a psychedelic drug experience, although Jimi himself claimed it was a love song. The lyrics "I'm acting funny and I don't know why / 'scuse me while I kiss the sky" seem to acknowledge at least some recreational pharmacology. In a similar vein, the Purple Haze shot, known equally well as the Purple Hooter, is meant to alter your reality for a little while. Constructed much like the Mind Eraser (see page 95), this layered shot is served on the rocks rather than in a shot glass.

THE NOTES

Place 6 or 7 square ice cubes into a rocks glass or a large shot glass. Pour in 1 fluid ounce (30ml) of citrus-flavored vodka, coating the ice. Take a long bar spoon and let the edge of the spoon touch just above the vodka. Slowly pour 1 fluid ounce (30ml) of raspberry liqueur, such as Chambord, over the back of the spoon to create a layer. Carefully add 1 fluid ounce (30ml) of lemon-lime soda. Drink as quickly as possible through a straw.

RED BARON

Manfred von Richthofen, better known as "the Red Baron," was a German fighter pilot during World War I. He was considered a hero of the German Air Force and earned his nickname from his family's status as *freiherr*," or "free lords," and from the bright red Fokker triplane he flew. The Red Baron shot honors von Richthofen's memory, by lighting a fire in the belly with vodka and orange juice, and adding that dash of red flair from the grenadine. The drink gives the appearance of a miniature sunrise, evocative of the Red Baron's dawn patrols over the Western Front.

THE NOTES

Pour ¾ fluid ounce (22.5ml) of vodka into a 1½ fluid ounce (45ml) shot glass. Add ¾ fluid ounce (22.5ml) of fresh orange juice and 1 splash of grenadine into the center of the glass, allowing it to settle to the bottom. This shot will look like a Tequila Sunrise cocktail, in miniature.

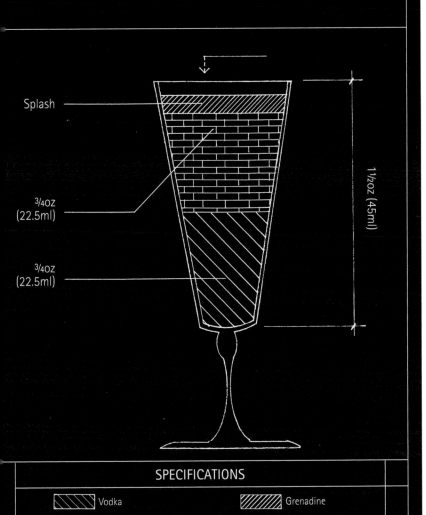

Splash

3/4OZ
(22.5ml)

3/4OZ
(22.5ml)

1½OZ (45ml)

SPECIFICATIONS

Vodka

Grenadine

Fresh orange juice

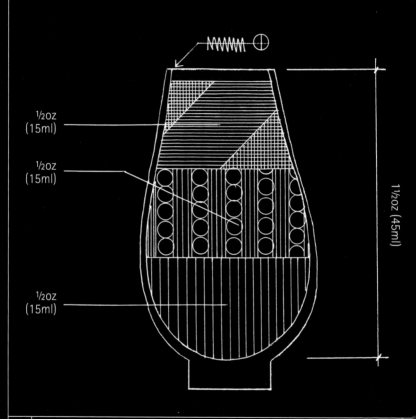

½OZ
(15ml)

½OZ
(15ml)

½OZ
(15ml)

1½oz (45ml)

SPECIFICATIONS

Bourbon

Fresh cranberry juice

Amaretto

RED SNAPPER

RED SNAPPER

Although the Red Snapper shot has the same name as a fish, it of course has nothing fishy about its components. The shot gets its name from the color of the cranberry juice and its "snap" from the bourbon. The red snapper fish is a popular game fish because of the fight it puts up while being reeled in. This shot is actually popular with fishing boat captains to celebrate their catch and honor the red snappers that are about to become dinner.

THE NOTES

Place 6 or 7 square ice cubes into a cocktail shaker. Pour in 3 fluid ounces (90ml) of bourbon, coating the ice. Add 3 fluid ounces (90ml) of amaretto and 3 fluid ounces (90ml) of fresh cranberry juice. Shake vigorously in a vertical motion for 10 seconds. Strain slowly into six 1½ fluid ounce (45ml) shot glasses.

SANTA

Father Christmas, St. Nicholas, Santa Claus, or Kris Kringle—whatever he may be called, he is the enduring symbol of the spirit of generosity and kindness shown at Christmas time. Santa has a long and storied history, and his appearance has changed many times over the years. The image most Western cultures recognize—that of the jolly white-bearded man in red—became popularized at the turn of the 20th century through various advertisements. First, by White Rock Beverages, and then most famously by the Coca-Cola Company. The Santa shot takes the popular red, green, and white colors associated with Santa and Christmas and translates them into festive layers in a shot glass.

THE NOTES

Pour ½ fluid ounce (15ml) of grenadine into a 1½ fluid ounce (45ml) shot glass. Take a long bar spoon and let the edge of the spoon touch just above the grenadine. Slowly pour ½ fluid ounce (15ml) of green crème de menthe over the back of the spoon to create a layer. Repeat this process with ½ fluid ounce (15ml) of peppermint schnapps to create a third and final layer.

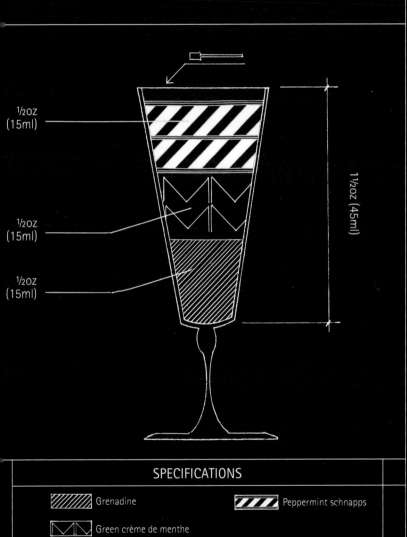

½oz
(15ml)

½oz
(15ml)

½oz
(15ml)

1½oz (45ml)

SPECIFICATIONS

Grenadine

Peppermint schnapps

Green crème de menthe

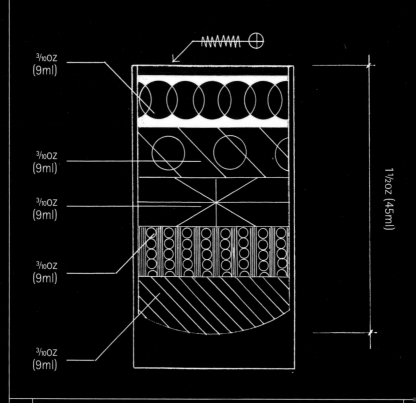

$^{3}/_{10}$OZ (9ml)

$^{3}/_{10}$OZ (9ml)

$^{3}/_{10}$OZ (9ml)

$^{3}/_{10}$OZ (9ml)

$^{3}/_{10}$OZ (9ml)

1½oz (45ml)

SPECIFICATIONS

Vodka

Amaretto

Irish cream liqueur

Triple sec

Heavy cream

SCREAMING TOE CURLER

In the world of shots, the word "screaming" is a prefix much like "mega" or "super." The shot is always stronger with the word "screaming" in front of it. Removing the coffee liqueur and adding vodka, triple sec, and heavy cream to a Toe Curler makes it a Screaming Toe Curler. To create any "screaming" shot, it's most common to float a small amount of vodka or bourbon on top. Another option to really heat things up is to float a small amount of overproof rum on top of a shot and set light to it before extinguishing and then drinking. The Screaming Toe Curler shot is strong but does not taste that way. After drinking it, a warm feeling will start to spread from your belly and make you want to curl your toes.

THE NOTES

Place 6 or 7 square ice cubes into a cocktail shaker. Pour in 1¾ fluid ounces (52.5ml) of vodka, coating the ice. Add 1¾ fluid ounces (52.5ml) of amaretto, 1¾ fluid ounces (52.5ml) of Irish cream liqueur, 1¾ fluid ounces (52.5ml) of triple sec, and 1¾ fluid ounces (52.5ml) of heavy cream. Shake vigorously in a vertical motion for 10 seconds. Strain slowly into six 1½ fluid ounce (45ml) shot glasses.

SILK PANTIES

Drinks with dirty names show up in many books and on web sites, but who is it that actually asks for them by name? The Silk Panties shot is less explicit than most other risqué drinks, but the name might still make you blush when ordering it from that cute bartender. It may not be a suitable shot to order when out for cocktails with the boss, but it would probably be a hit at the next bachelor or bachelorette party. The silky texture of the peach schnapps combines with vodka to make a shot that is powerfully strong and alcoholic. The drinker should beware: any shot that is half vodka can pack quite a punch.

THE NOTES

Place 6 or 7 square ice cubes into a cocktail shaker. Pour in 4½ fluid ounces (135ml) of vodka, coating the ice. Add 4½ fluid ounces (135ml) of peach schnapps. Shake vigorously in a vertical motion for 10 seconds. Strain slowly into six 1½ fluid ounce (45ml) shot glasses.

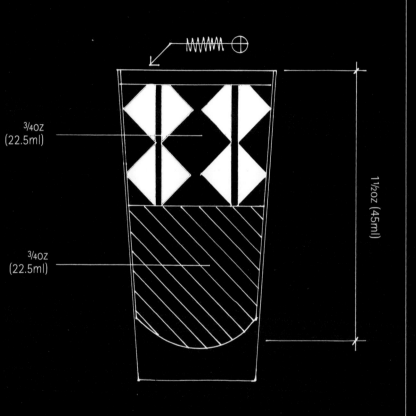

³/₄OZ (22.5ml)

³/₄OZ (22.5ml)

1½oz (45ml)

SPECIFICATIONS

Vodka

Peach schnapps

SILK PANTIES 115

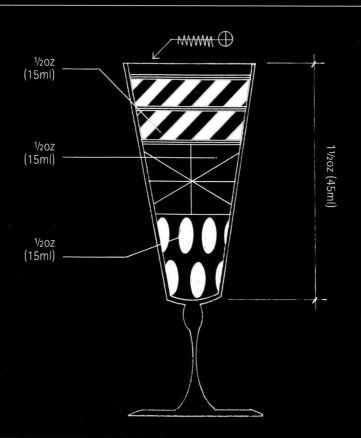

½OZ
(15ml)

½OZ
(15ml)

½OZ
(15ml)

1½oz (45ml)

SPECIFICATIONS

((()) Coffee liqueur

⧄⧄⧄ Peppermint schnapps

⊠⊠ Irish cream liqueur

SLIPPERY SLOPE

SLIPPERY SLOPE

The earliest known usage of the phrase "slippery slope" is from an 1888 poem by Will Henry Thompson, *High Tide at Gettysburg*: "They smote and stood, who held the hope / Of nations on that slippery slope." In this case it was a literal reference to a hillside that had become slippery with blood. The *Oxford English Dictionary* first listed the words "slippery slope" in 1951, to mean an action that will lead inexorably from one action to another with unintended consequences. How appropriate then that the name of this shot is Slippery Slope, a heady mix of coffee liqueur, Irish cream, and peppermint schnapps that, if imbibed in large quantities, is almost sure to start you down the slippery slope of having another, and another, and another!

THE NOTES

Place 6 or 7 square ice cubes into a cocktail shaker. Pour in 3 fluid ounces (90ml) of coffee liqueur, coating the ice. Add 3 fluid ounces (90ml) of Irish cream liqueur and 3 fluid ounces (90ml) of peppermint schnapps. Shake vigorously in a vertical motion for 10 seconds. Strain slowly into six 1½ fluid ounce (45ml) shot glasses.

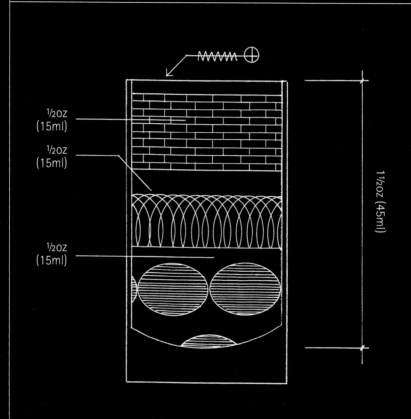

½oz
(15ml)

½oz
(15ml)

½oz
(15ml)

1½oz (45ml)

SPECIFICATIONS

Sloe gin

Fresh orange juice

Southern Comfort

SLOE COMFORTABLE SCREW

SLOE COMFORTABLE SCREW

The name of this shot is really not as dirty as it may seem, since it actually describes the drink, albeit with a double entendre that was surely intentional. The Sloe Comfortable Screw is simply a screwdriver made with sloe gin and Southern Comfort, instead of vodka. Sloe drupes are the small, hard fruit of the blackthorn or sloe shrub. Gin is infused with the fruit and sugar added to produce a red liqueur called sloe gin. Sloe gin is a popular homemade liqueur in Great Britain, with several competitions held annually to determine the best-tasting product. Variations of sloe gin can also be found in Germany, where the gin is replaced by white rum, and in Spain anise-flavored brandy is used instead.

THE NOTES

Place 6 or 7 square ice cubes into a cocktail shaker. Pour in 3 fluid ounces (90ml) of sloe gin, coating the ice. Add 3 fluid ounces (90ml) of Southern Comfort and 3 fluid ounces (90ml) of fresh orange juice. Shake vigorously in a vertical motion for 10 seconds. Strain slowly into six 1½ fluid ounce (45ml) shot glasses.

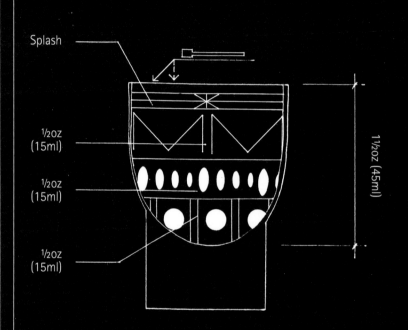

Splash

½oz (15ml)

½oz (15ml)

½oz (15ml)

1½oz (45ml)

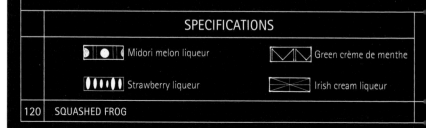

SPECIFICATIONS

Midori melon liqueur   Green crème de menthe

Strawberry liqueur   Irish cream liqueur

SQUASHED FROG

This shot's evocative name should by now be an indicator that it might not be the most pleasant experience. It tastes quite delicious, but sadly, it does look very much like a squashed frog. The same reaction that creates the Cement Mixer (see page 43) and Brain/Bloody Brain (see page 39) is at work in this drink. The Irish cream liqueur starts to curdle in the presence of the acidic mixer, creating a lumpy, green-and-red horror show that clings to the throat as it goes down. The only redeeming virtue of this drink is the fact that the Midori melon liqueur and strawberry liqueur go together surprisingly well, so once the shot is downed, the overall impression is less awful than expected.

THE NOTES

Pour ½ fluid ounce (15ml) of Midori melon liqueur into a 1½ fluid ounce (45ml) shot glass. Take a long bar spoon and let the edge of the spoon touch just above the Midori. Slowly pour ½ fluid ounce (15ml) of strawberry liqueur over the back of the spoon to create a layer. Repeat this process with ½ fluid ounce (15ml) of the green crème de menthe to create a third and final layer. Carefully add 1 splash of Irish cream liqueur into the center of the drink for the full "curdled-milk" effect.

STOPLIGHT

The first traffic control signal to use lights was installed outside the British Houses of Parliament in London, England. The device used a gas lamp with red and green lenses and was controlled by a policeman who would manually turn it to change the signal. In 1912, Lester Wire, an American policeman in Salt Lake City, Utah, created a similar device using electric lights, which proved to be much safer than gas. The colors of the lights matched the colors used for railroad signals at the time—green for go and red for stop, with yellow being added in between in the 1920s. The shot follows the same color pattern: green, yellow, red.

THE NOTES

Pour 3 fluid ounces (90ml) of vodka equally between three 1½ fluid ounce (45ml) shot glasses. Add ½ fluid ounce (15ml) of Midori melon liqueur to one glass, ½ fluid ounce (15ml) of fresh orange juice to the second glass, and ½ fluid ounce (15ml) of fresh cranberry juice to the third glass. Drink them successively: green, yellow, and red.

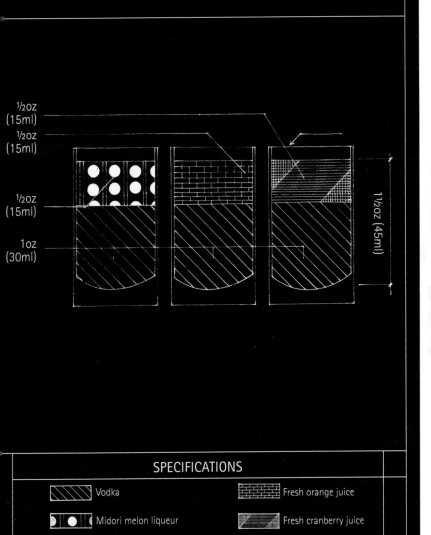

½oz
(15ml)

½oz
(15ml)

½oz
(15ml)

1oz
(30ml)

1½oz (45ml)

SPECIFICATIONS

Vodka

Fresh orange juice

Midori melon liqueur

Fresh cranberry juice

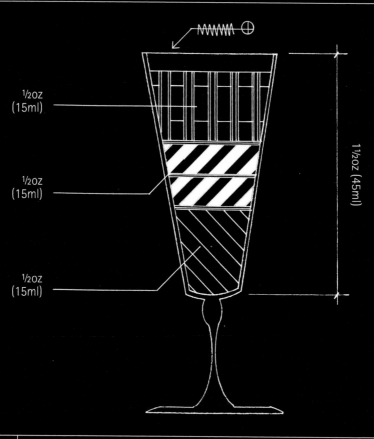

½oz
(15ml)

½oz
(15ml)

½oz
(15ml)

1½oz (45ml)

SPECIFICATIONS

Vodka

Blue curaçao

Peppermint schnapps

SUBZERO

The key to the Subzero shot is a protein called the "transient receptor potential caution channel subfamily M member 8" (TRPM8). TRPM8 is a type of protein called an ion channel, and it works like a key in a lock. TRPM8 opens in the presence of cold temperatures, allowing ions to enter the cells in our taste buds, by which we can sense the cold. TRPM8 is a protein that can, however, be fooled by several naturally occurring oils, including eucalyptus and menthol. Menthol causes TRPM8 to send the same cold signal that an actual temperature change would have sent, tricking our senses into feeling cold when it is not there. The menthol in the peppermint schnapps provides the cooling effect of the Subzero shot, and the blue curaçao and vodka give its "ice blue" appearance.

THE NOTES

Place 6 or 7 square ice cubes into a cocktail shaker. Pour in 3 fluid ounces (90ml) of vodka, coating the ice. Add 3 fluid ounces (90ml) of peppermint schnapps and 3 fluid ounces (90ml) of blue curaçao. Shake vigorously in a vertical motion for 10 seconds. Strain slowly into six 1½ fluid ounce (45ml) shot glasses.

THREE WISE MEN

In Christian Nativity scenes, the three wise men, or magi, present their gifts of gold, frankincense, and myrrh to the baby Jesus, symbolizing the recognition of Jesus as king. However, a gathering of three wise men is not a scene that is limited to Christian theology. For example, the word "tribunal" comes from the fact that there would typically be three judges listening to the plaintiff's case. For the Three Wise Men shot, some of the most esteemed "men" in the world of alcoholic beverages have been gathered together. Each of these whiskeys—one Scotch and two American—holds a long and distinguished history. Meet Johnnie, Jack, and Jim.

THE NOTES

Pour ½ fluid ounce (15ml) of each whiskey into a 1½ fluid ounce (45ml) shot glass.
A popular variation of this shot is Three Wise Men Go Hunting, which sees the addition of Wild Turkey whiskey to the three listed here.

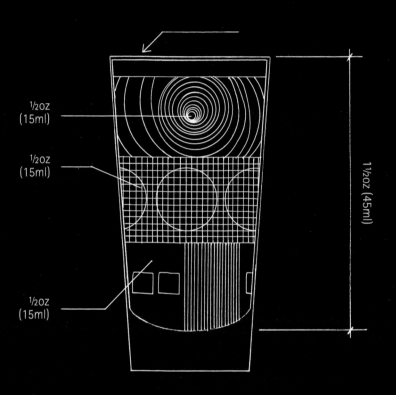

½oz
(15ml)

½oz
(15ml)

½oz
(15ml)

1½oz (45ml)

SPECIFICATIONS

Jack Daniel's

Johnnie Walker

Jim Beam

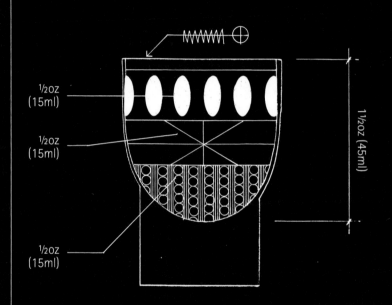

½oz
(15ml)

½oz
(15ml)

½oz
(15ml)

1½oz (45ml)

SPECIFICATIONS

Amaretto

Irish cream liqueur

Coffee liqueur

128   TOE CURLER

TOE CURLER

Kahlúa is by far the most popular and well-known brand of coffee liqueur, but another less well-known and arguably superior brand is Tia Maria. Coffee liqueur is made by infusing a base spirit with an intensely concentrated brewed coffee and other flavorings, such as cocoa and vanilla. For both Kahlúa and Tia Maria, the base spirit is rum, but for other brands it can be a neutral spirit such as vodka or even brandy. After the infusion is complete, the liqueur is sweetened with sugar and mixed with water to bring it to the target alcohol content. Coffee liqueur is an essential ingredient in many of the shots in this book and especially the Toe Curler. The coffee liqueur in the shot provides a dark, rich coffee flavor that enhances the sweet amaretto and Irish cream. As with the screaming variation, prepare for the ensuing warmth to spread from belly to toes.

THE NOTES

Place 6 or 7 square ice cubes into a cocktail shaker. Pour in 3 fluid ounces (90ml) of amaretto, coating the ice. Add 3 fluid ounces (90ml) of Irish cream liqueur and 3 fluid ounces (90ml) of coffee liqueur. Shake vigorously in a vertical motion for 10 seconds. Strain slowly into six 1½ fluid ounce (45ml) shot glasses.

TOMAHAWK

Before Europeans came to North America, the natives would use sharpened stones attached to wooden handles for common uses such as chopping, hunting, or combat. In the Powhatan language, they were called *tamahaac*, which was later anglicized to "tomahawk." The word "tomahawk" may originally come from the Native American axe, but this shot's name comes from the cruise missile of the same name used by the United States Navy. The Tomahawk missile is known for its accuracy and impact, although it is not very fast. The Tomahawk shot, likewise, may take a while to kick in because the chocolate, heavy cream, and lime juice mask the effects of the vodka. But once that vodka hits its target, the name starts to make sense.

THE NOTES

Place 6 or 7 square ice cubes into a cocktail shaker. Pour in 1¾ fluid ounces (52.5ml) of vodka, coating the ice. Add 1¾ fluid ounces (52.5ml) of chocolate liqueur, 1¾ fluid ounces (52.5ml) of triple sec, 1¾ fluid ounces (52.5ml) of fresh lime juice, and 1¾ fluid ounces (52.5ml) of heavy cream. Shake vigorously in a vertical motion for 10 seconds. Strain slowly into six 1½ fluid ounce (45ml) shot glasses.

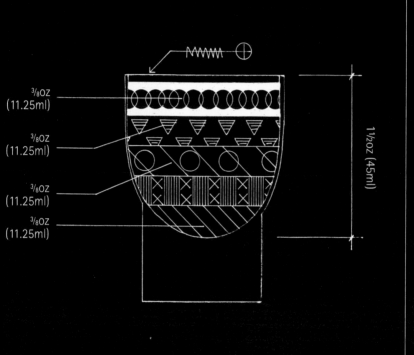

³/₈OZ
(11.25ml)

³/₈OZ
(11.25ml)

³/₈OZ
(11.25ml)

³/₈OZ
(11.25ml)

1½oz (45ml)

SPECIFICATIONS

Vodka	Fresh lime juice
Chocolate liqueur	Heavy cream
Triple sec	

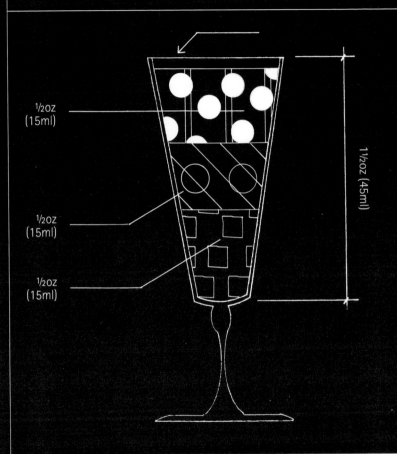

½oz
(15ml)

½oz
(15ml)

½oz
(15ml)

1½oz (45ml)

SPECIFICATIONS

Jägermeister

Overproof rum

Triple sec

UNDERTAKER

Just as some shots have dirty or risqué names, there are shots with deadly sounding names, and the Undertaker is just one of those (see also Voodoo on page 135 and Hand Grenade on page 72). The defining characteristic of "deadly" shots is a taste that might charitably be called harsh. Many people are afraid of Jägermeister because of its mysterious ingredients and strong, medicinal flavor. The Undertaker shot will be seen by some as a test of strength and courage, as it combines Jägermeister with overproof rum. The Jägermeister and rum in this shot are actually tempered by the triple sec, and the overall flavor is a rather pleasant combination of orange and licorice. But do not be fooled! This shot is very strong and should be consumed with caution and in moderation.

THE NOTES

Pour ½ fluid ounce (15ml) of Jägermeister into a 1½ fluid ounce (45ml) shot glass. Add ½ fluid ounce (15ml) of triple sec and ½ fluid ounce (15ml) of overproof rum.

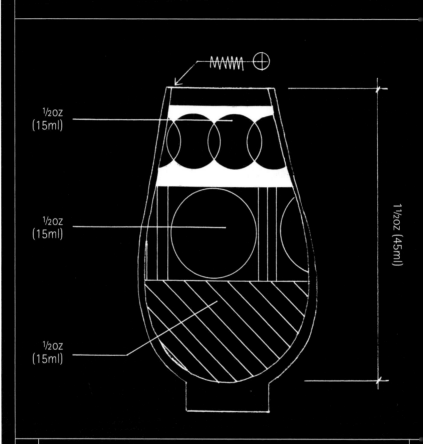

½oz
(15ml)

½oz
(15ml)

½oz
(15ml)

1½oz (45ml)

SPECIFICATIONS

Vodka

Heavy cream

Black sambuca

VOODOO

New Orleans Voodoo arose out of the slave trade as an amalgamation of African traditions, Creole culture, and French Catholic beliefs, all of which merged into a set of spiritual folklore and rituals. New Orleans Voodoo introduced to popular culture items such as Voodoo dolls and Gris-Gris, which are charms or amulets meant to protect the wearer from evil spirits or bad luck. New Orleans is also famous in the United States as the primary source of the French spirit absinthe, up until it was banned in 1912. Absinthe was thought to give the drinker visions and phantom sensations that combined well with Voodoo rituals. The Voodoo shot may not actually cause you to see visions, but the anise flavor of the absinthe combined with the soothing coolness of the cream can help you to, as they say in 'Nawlins, "*Laissez les bons temps rouler!*" (Let the good times roll!) Absinthe was made legal again in the United States in 2007, and New Orleans is once again starting to produce it. If absinthe cannot be found, black sambuca, ouzo, or pastis can be used in its place.

THE NOTES

Place 6 or 7 square ice cubes into a cocktail shaker. Pour in 3 fluid ounces (90ml) of vodka, coating the ice. Add 3 fluid ounces (90ml) of black sambuca and 3 fluid ounces (90ml) of heavy cream. Shake vigorously in a vertical motion for 10 seconds. Strain slowly into six 1½ fluid ounce (45ml) shot glasses.

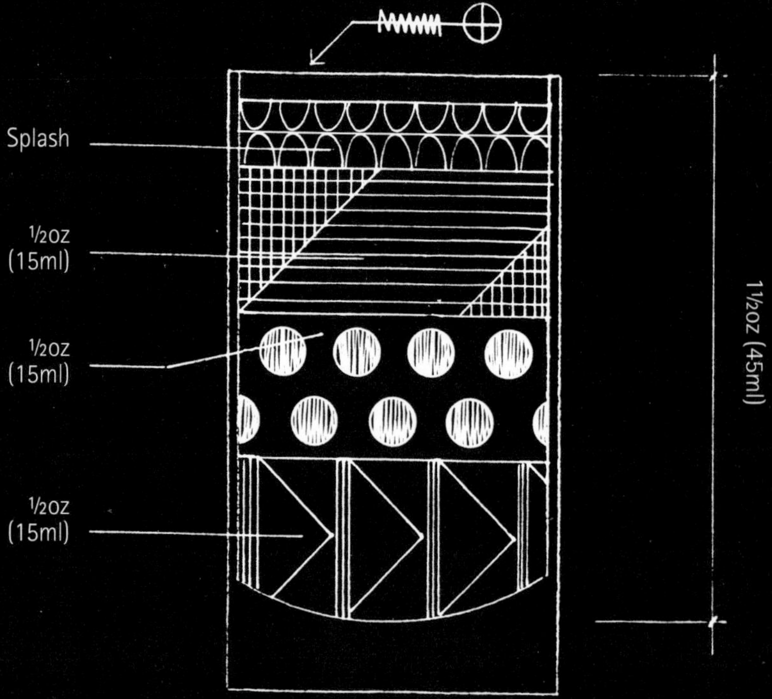

Splash

½oz
(15ml)

½oz
(15ml)

½oz
(15ml)

1½oz (45ml)

SPECIFICATIONS

Canadian whiskey

Sour apple liqueur

Fresh cranberry juice

Lemon-lime soda

WASHINGTON APPLE

Washington State on the western coast of the United States is one of the largest producers of apples in the world. Washington State currently has over 175,000 acres of apple orchards, with the Red Delicious variety accounting for more than 30 percent of all production. The high elevation and rich lava ash soil of the Cascade Mountains make Washington State an ideal area for large-scale apple production. All of this makes it a shame that the Washington Apple shot tarnishes the state's apple-based pride by combining a Canadian (shudder) whiskey with the "greener than it has any right to be" Apple Pucker, a sour green apple liqueur. Canadian whiskey uses rye and corn grains, making it smoother and lighter than other whiskies, a flavor that works best with the sweet ingredients in this shot.

THE NOTES

Place 6 or 7 square ice cubes into a cocktail shaker. Pour in 3 fluid ounces (90ml) of Canadian whiskey, such as Crown Royal, coating the ice. Add 3 fluid ounces (90ml) of sour apple liqueur, such as Apple Pucker, and 3 fluid ounces (90ml) of fresh cranberry juice. Shake vigorously in a vertical motion for 10 seconds. Strain slowly into six 1½ fluid ounce (45ml) shot glasses, filling each about two-thirds full. Top off each shot glass with a splash of lemon-lime soda.

WINDEX

Windex is a cleaning solution used primarily on glass. Invented in 1933 by Harry R. Drackett, it has been reformulated several times because the original formulation was almost 100 percent solvents. The product is sold in a variety of colors, but best known is the iconic blue. The Windex shot is made blue by the addition of blue curaçao. The potency of the cleaning product may also help explain why this shot got its name.

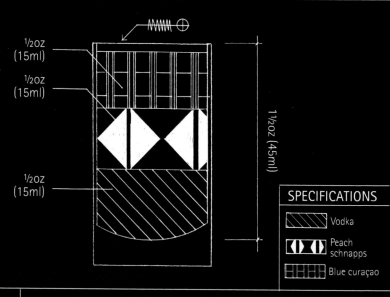

1/2oz (15ml)

1/2oz (15ml)

1/2oz (15ml)

1 1/2oz (45ml)

SPECIFICATIONS

- Vodka
- Peach schnapps
- Blue curaçao

THE NOTES

Place 6 or 7 square ice cubes into a cocktail shaker. Pour in 3 fluid ounces (90ml) of vodka, coating the ice. Add 3 fluid ounces (90ml) of peach schnapps and 3 fluid ounces (90ml) of blue curaçao. Shake vigorously in a vertical motion for 10 seconds. Strain slowly into six 1½ fluid ounce (45ml) shot glasses.

WOO WOO

According to many dubious sources, "woo woo" is a derogatory term for ideas based on little or no evidence, or the occult. It can also used to describe someone who is excited—which may apply to this shot. The Woo Woo is both tasty and extremely simple to make, with busy bartenders.

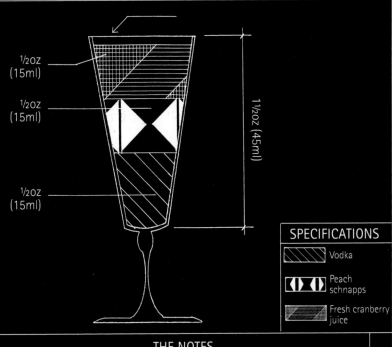

½oz
(15ml)

½oz
(15ml)

½oz
(15ml)

1½oz (45ml)

SPECIFICATIONS

Vodka

Peach schnapps

Fresh cranberry juice

THE NOTES

Place 6 or 7 square ice cubes into a cocktail shaker. Pour in 3 fluid ounces (90ml) of vodka, coating the ice. Add 3 fluid ounces (90ml) of peach schnapps and 3 fluid ounces (90ml) of fresh cranberry juice. Shake vigorously in a vertical motion for 10 seconds. Strain slowly into six 1½ fluid ounce (45ml) shot glasses.

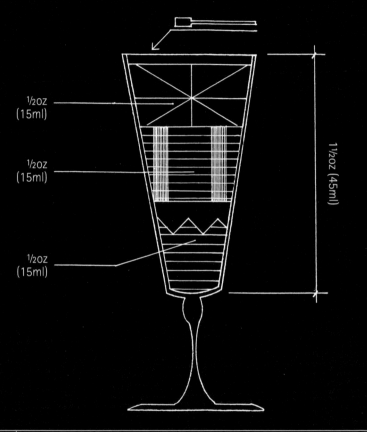

½oz (15ml)

½oz (15ml)

½oz (15ml)

1½oz (45ml)

SPECIFICATIONS

Grand Marnier

Irish cream liqueur

Tequila

ZIPPER

The zipper as we know it today was invented by Whitcomb Judson in 1893. The name "zipper" was first used by the B. F. Goodrich Company in 1923, when they used Sundback's design on their rubber boots. The name described both the sound the new fastener made and the speed at which it worked. The smooth cognac in the Grand Marnier gives the shot a sweet orange flavor that combines well with the silky chocolate flavor of the Irish cream. The real "zip" comes in when the white tequila is added, bringing a bright, hot, raw flavor that, like a zipper, pulls the shot together.

THE NOTES

Pour ½ fluid ounce (15ml) of Grand Marnier into a 1½ fluid ounce (45ml) shot glass. Take a long bar spoon and let the edge of the spoon touch just above the Grand Marnier. Slowly pour ½ fluid ounce (15ml) of tequila over the back of the spoon to create a layer. Repeat this process with ½ fluid ounce (15ml) of Irish cream liqueur, to create a third and final layer.

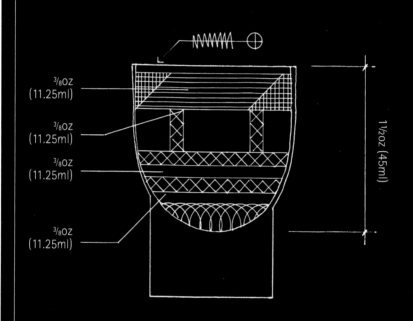

³/₈OZ
(11.25ml)

³/₈OZ
(11.25ml)

³/₈OZ
(11.25ml)

³/₈OZ
(11.25ml)

1½oz (45ml)

SPECIFICATIONS

Southern Comfort

Apricot brandy

Blackberry liqueur

Fresh cranberry juice

ZOOT SUIT RIOT

In 1943, there was a series of riots in Los Angeles dubbed the Zoot Suit Riots. The fights were between white servicemen on leave during World War II and the local Mexican-American population. The zoot suits that the Mexican gangs wore at the time were thought to be unpatriotic, both because of their association with crime, as well as their open flaunting of rationing laws. "Zoot Suit Riot" is also the name of a modern swing song, released in 1997 by the band Cherry Poppin' Daddies—the lyrics in the song refer to events in the riots. The modern swing revival led to the creation of the Zoot Suit Riot shot. Swing dancing requires a lot of energy, and this shot provides it, with two sugar- and antioxidant-rich fruit juices. The dancing also requires a fair amount of courage, and the Southern Comfort and brandy provide that in liquid form.

THE NOTES

Place 6 or 7 square ice cubes into a cocktail shaker. Pour in 2¼ fluid ounces (67.5ml) of Southern Comfort, coating the ice. Add 2¼ fluid ounces (67.5ml) of apricot brandy, 2¼ fluid ounces (67.5ml) of blackberry liqueur, and 2¼ fluid ounces (67.5ml) of fresh cranberry juice. Shake vigorously in a vertical motion for 10 seconds. Strain slowly into six 1½ fluid ounce (45ml) shot glasses.

To Jill and to my children, Camryn, Colby, and Cooper.—PK

For Noel, Hallie, and Corey—here's looking at you, kids.—MW

ABOUT THE AUTHOR/ILLUSTRATOR

PAUL KNORR iis the author of a number of books on cocktails, shots, and shooters and is the creator of Barback, a drink recipe software program for organizing recipes. His favorite shots are the Alaskan Pipeline and the Bazooka Joe.

MELISSA WOOD is an illustrator, designer, and architectural aficionado who pored over Charles Addams' and James Thurber's cartoons as a child and dreamed of one day illustrating a book of her own. Melissa has three terrific children and makes a wicked Bloody Mary.